herbaceous.

herbaceous.

a cook's guide to culinary herbs

IAN AND ELIZABETH HEMPHILL WITH PHILIPPA SANDALL

Photography by Greg Elms

conran
OCTOPUS

Acknowledgments

Our sincere thanks and gratitude to John and Rosemary Hemphill for generously sharing the intellectual property of their many books, particularly *What Herb Is That?*

We would also like to thank Lansdowne Publishing for providing us with many of the original herb images from *Herbs, Their Cultivation and Usage*; Roger, Richard and Emma Sandall for their keyboard skills in helping set up the database; Foong Ling Kong of Hardie Grant, Klarissa Pfisterer and Hamish Freeman for creating such a beautiful book.

Grateful acknowledgement is due to the following for permission to reuse their recipes in this book: Basil variations from Amy Nathan (*Openers*, Chronicle Books, San Francisco, 1988); Bay leaf sorbet from Anthony Gardiner (*Herbes de Provence*, New Holland, 2002); Kalamata olives with fennel and basil from Lucio Galleto and Timothy Fisher (*The Art of Food at Lucio's*, Craftsman House, 1999); Vietnamese chicken with lemongrass from Charmaine Solomon (*The Complete Asian Cookbook*, New Holland, 2002); Mitsuba and tofu in clear soup from Hideo Dekura; Coconut rice cooked in pandan leaves, Pandan-flavoured coconut pancakes and Whiting fillets grilled in turmeric leaves from Carol Selva Rajah; Goat's cheese soufflés from Anneka Manning (*More Good Food*, Text Publishing, 2000); and Snowpea, rocket, capsicum, avocado and basil salad from Lisa Lintner.

The authors and publishers would like to thank MINIMAX for their help with the loan of props.

References

Hemphill, Ian, *Spice Notes*, Macmillan, Sydney, 2000
Hemphill, John and Rosemary, *What Herb Is That?* Lansdowne, Sydney, 1995
Hemphill, John and Rosemary, *Herbs, Their Cultivation and Usage,* Lansdowne, Sydney, 1993
Hemphill, Rosemary, *Fragrance & Flavour* (revised edition), Hardie Grant Books, Melbourne, 2002

This edition published in 2004 by Conran Octopus Limited,
a part of Octopus Publishing Group, 2–4 Heron Quays, London E14 4JP
www.conran-octopus.co.uk

British Cataloguing-in-Publication Data.
A catalogue record for this book is available from the British Library

ISBN 1 84091 381 9

First published in 2003 by Hardie Grant Books
12 Claremont Street, South Yarra, Victoria 3141, Australia, www.hardiegrant.com.au

Co-written with Philippa Sandall
Photography by Greg Elms
Styling by Celia Dowzer
Designed and typeset by
Hamish Freeman & Klarissa Pfisterer
Printed and bound in Singapore by Imago

10 9 8 7 6 5 4 3 2 1

For our three daughters,
Catherine, Margaret and Sophie

contents

introduction

When I was young and my parents were busy introducing Australians to herbs other than parsley and mint, we were often amused to notice how humble our plants appeared to be in the eyes of many horticulturalists when compared with their 'superb' ornamental trees and shrubs and 'magnificent, prize-winning' blooms.

But our quiet amusement has turned into deep satisfaction over the years as Australians, like herb-lovers the world over, have taken herbs and all they give us to heart and now grow them, cook with them and use them in natural therapies.

Liz and I married young (just before our 21st birthdays), and we worked alongside my parents (Rosemary and John) at Dural for some 16 years cultivating and marketing the 'Somerset Cottage' range of herbs and spices. In between raising three daughters, Liz helped out by making rosemary scones and serving tea to the endless bus groups who stopped by to learn about growing and using culinary herbs (we were on the 'talk/herb garden tour/tea' route). Liz also made and sold thousands of sleep pillows filled with lavender, lemon verbena and rose petals which she had somehow found time to harvest and dry.

In 1975 she decided to share some of her own experiences and wrote a book for children called *Your First Book of Herb Gardening*. Many of its greatest fans, however, turned out to be adults, who appreciated Liz's down-to-earth approach and her whimsical humour. Now, while working with me at 'Herbies' Spices' in Rozelle, Sydney, Liz and our long-time friend, Philippa Sandall, have trawled Mum and Dad's most comprehensive work, *What Herb is That?* to bring it up to date for a new generation of herb lovers. Hence *Herbaceous: A cook's guide to culinary herbs*.

Dip into *Herbaceous* and you will learn about all the culinary herbs you can find in your local garden centre or buy in fresh bunches from fruit and vegetable retailers, as well as ways to use them, recipes and tips on growing them. We have divided the book into three parts. The story begins with my section on 'Herb Essentials' – all those things you wanted to know about culinary herbs but were never game to ask. 'Is it a herb or a spice?', 'Should I use it fresh or dried?', 'Can I freeze it?', 'Why do I have to store it in a cupboard and not stack it in a neat row in my nice wall spice rack?'

We tell you what you need to know about herbs to get the best out of them, such as information about harvesting, preparing, freezing, drying and storing.

Liz picks up the baton for the bulk of the book in the second section, The Herbs – with all you need to know about using and growing 50 popular culinary herbs along with some pretty mouth-watering recipes and tips on which herbs are used for what cuisine.

Last but not least, I get 'Down to Earth' and pass on the secrets that my 'green-fingered' Dad shared with me about growing herbs successfully. I discuss the equipment you will need, where you can grow herbs and how to plant, propagate, prune and look after them.

Our family has been learning about, using and growing herbs for over 50 years and we hope you will be fascinated and inspired by these wonderful plants that give so much satisfaction from seemingly such little effort.

Ian Hemphill, Sydney, 2003

herb essentials

WHAT ARE HERBS?

So just what are herbs? For those of us who use them regularly, we generally refer to the leaf of a plant that we use in cooking as a culinary herb and any other part of the plant that is most often dried, as a spice.

Spices can come from all sorts of parts of plants, ranging from dried, unopened flower buds in the case of cloves, to the bark of a tropical evergreen tree for cinnamon.

Sections of roots of plants, often referred to as rhizomes, give us spices like ginger, turmeric and galangal. Berries from trees, shrubs and vines are gathered and dried to create allspice, barberries and peppercorns. Even the stigma of a particular purple-flowered crocus is plucked in the case of saffron. The aromatic seeds of many herb plants are gathered and dried to give a vast array of seed spices, including fennel, dill, caraway, anise and cumin.

Many of the aromatic seeds we call spices are actually gathered from herb plants when they have finished flowering. A familiar example is coriander: the leaves are referred to as a herb, however the dried seeds are always called a spice.

So now you may ask, 'what about the stem and roots of coriander that are used in cooking, and what about onions, garlic and the delicious bulb of fennel?' These sections of vegetable material, that are mostly used fresh to enhance the flavour of food, tend to be classified with herbs. Therefore when a cook is adding ingredients such as coriander leaves, lemongrass stalk, garlic and coriander roots these may all be referred to as the herbs. The cumin, pepper, chilli, galangal and ginger will probably be referred to as the spices.

FRESH OR DRIED?

An important characteristic of most spices is that they are generally used in their dried form.

Many herbs, on the other hand, tend to be used when they are fresh, because those herbs with delicate fragrances and highly volatile 'top notes' only contain their truly aromatic attributes when they are fresh.

'Fresh' is a word that is much bandied around these days and is often used in different contexts, which can be confusing. Freshness is always critical in the context of being 'ready to consume' or 'not old and tasteless'. However when we say 'fresh herbs' the term means herbs that have been freshly picked, and have not been dried, frozen or processed in any way.

In some cases the fresh item is clearly best, for instance basil, coriander, rocket and Vietnamese mint leaves are among many herbs that are significantly better when fresh. Having said this, when deciding to use a fresh or dried herb you do need to consider which is more appropriate for its particular application.

For centuries people have been drying the different varieties of herbs and spices for varying reasons, the most common being that it preserves them in a storable form for later use, when either the crop is not available or is not conveniently to hand when it is required.

With the majority of spices, the drying or curing process creates certain enzymatic reactions within the spice itself, and this in turn creates the distinctive flavour we are looking for. It is what produces the uniquely different flavours of spices such as vanilla, cloves, pepper and allspice. For example, the drying of peppercorns in the sun turns them black and forms the volatile oil piperine, which gives pepper its unique taste. Before curing, the vanilla bean is a green, tasteless, odourless bean that grows on a tropical, climbing orchid.

Another reason for drying herbs that is often overlooked, is to have them in a form that imparts the flavour most effectively into the food being cooked.

An example would be to try and make a cup of peppermint tea with fresh peppermint leaves. The result would be an infusion with very little flavour and a low level of the therapeutic volatile oils in the tea. However, the drying and processing of peppermint leaves makes them infuse readily with hot water to make an effective cup of herbal tea, with the characteristic flavour we know so well. The infusion would be comparatively bland and entirely different if made with fresh peppermint leaves.

The same principle applies to cooking with herbs such as thyme, sage, marjoram, oregano and bay leaves.

DRYING YOUR OWN HERBS

It is not difficult to dry your own herbs and it is possible to achieve a professional result when a few logical guidelines are followed.

Firstly, herbs will dry best when you pick your own fresh from the garden. Bunches that have been kept in cold storage or transported for long distances after harvesting will often develop spots of discoloration on the leaves, caused by oxidisation or partial fermenting.

Next, if picking your own, remember to gather your herbs in the morning, just after the dew has dried and before the heat of the day has reduced their pungency.

The traditional method of drying is to tie up the stems of the herbs into bunches about the size of a small feather duster. Hang these bunches in a dark, warm, dry and well-aired place for up to a week. When the leaves feel perfectly crisp and dry, strip them off the stems and store them in an airtight container. If the leaves feel at all soft or leathery, they are not dry enough and will go mouldy.

If you are very keen, it is not difficult to make drying frames about half a metre (about 20 in) square and 10 cm (4 in) deep with a fine mesh insect screen stretched across the base.

The herbs should be spread out in the frames to an approximate depth of 2 cm (¾ in), and then placed in a dark, well-aired place where the air can circulate freely around them. It is important to note that the herbs will dry faster if the leaves are removed from the stems first. The leaves dry more quickly on their own because you are not trying to remove the moisture from the thicker stems at the same time.

I have actually experienced a phenomenon when perfectly dry leaves were left on the stem for a couple of days after drying. The moisture in the not-so-dry woody stems migrated back into the dry leaves and they had to be dried for a bit longer after being stripped off.

Every herb has its own structural characteristics and so each type of herb will dry a little differently to another. Leaf size, density, moisture content and a host of physical attributes will cause each individual herb to yield up its water content in different ways, so you will always need to feel for that tell-tale crunchy texture of a properly dried herb.

It is also possible to dry herbs in conventional and microwave ovens. To dry herbs in a conventional oven bring the heat to about 120°C (250°F). Place herb leaves that have been removed from their stems in a single layer on a baking tray lined with greaseproof paper. Place them in the oven, turn off the heat and crack the door just open. After half an hour, remove the tray of herbs, reheat the oven to 120°C (250°F) and repeat the process. Keep repeating the process until the leaves are crisp and dry.

When drying herbs in a microwave oven you need to be careful not to kill the magnetron, which is something that can happen when there is not enough moisture to absorb the microwaves. Place the picked herb leaves on a sheet of paper towel in the microwave oven with a microwave-safe cup, half full of water. Zap the leaves for 20 seconds on high and then remove any dry, crisp leaves. Keep zapping in 10-second bursts until they are all dry, continually removing the dried leaves. You won't damage your oven because even when all but a few leaves have been taken out, the water in the cup will still absorb the microwaves.

When a herb is dried, most of the water content is removed leaving the dried, shrivelled leaf still containing the essential oils that give the herb its flavour. Because the dried herb is like a concentrated form of the fresh, a general rule of thumb for recipes is to use one-quarter to one-third of the dried quantity that you would have included of fresh.

STORING DRIED HERBS

Optimum storage conditions for your own dried herbs, or ones you have bought already dried, will mean that they can be kept ready to use for up to 18 months or more.

Dried herbs should be kept in airtight packaging to retain their essential oils and to prevent excessive exposure to the air that will cause the oils to oxidise more rapidly and lose their pungency.

The packs must be kept away from extremes of heat, light and humidity. This is because heat will evaporate the herb's volatile components and the flavour will deteriorate.

A spice rack might look attractive in one's kitchen, however unless it is used to store the herbs and spices you use regularly, excessive light from fluorescent tubes or direct sunlight pouring in through a kitchen window will bleach out colour and flavour will be lost at the same time.

Humidity is another major enemy of effective dried herb storage. A rise in humidity brings with it extra moisture, and the result of that is faster deterioration of flavour. Never store dried herbs in the refrigerator. When a pack is taken out of the cold environment, condensation will form. The condensation introduces more moisture that will shorten the storage life of dried herbs.

STORING FRESH HERBS

Believe it or not, there are many ways you can get the most from those bunches of fresh herbs you buy, and never seem to use entirely in one hit.

Most soft-leaf herbs such as basil, chervil, coriander, dill, parsley and tarragon may be kept for up to a week in a glass of water in the refrigerator. Wash them in clean, cold water first and make sure the bottom 2.5 cm (1 in) of the stems are immersed in water, then cover the foliage, snood-like, with a clean plastic bag.

Herbs with harder stems and more robust foliage, such as thyme, sage, marjoram and rosemary, may be kept in a glass of water in the kitchen and need not be refrigerated.

Whether storing in the refrigerator or not, try to remember to change the water every couple of days.

FREEZING FRESH HERBS

You can freeze many herbs when you need a longer storage period.

Hard-stemmed herbs store well when sprigs are wrapped in foil and placed in a freezer bag in the freezer.

A convenient method for freezing softer herbs is in ice-cube trays. Chop the herb finely – with a herb like coriander where we use all of the plant, chop the leaves, stems and roots – then fill sections of an ice-cube tray two-thirds full with chopped herb, just cover with water and freeze. When frozen, turn out the herb-cubes and store them in a freezer bag. You need to keep the frozen herbs in freezer bags, otherwise they may pick up unwanted aromas from other foods stored alongside them.

WHEN TO USE FRESH OR DRIED HERBS

There are many dishes where we would say it is preferable to use fresh herbs to get the true effect. For example in Thai cooking, fresh coriander leaves, ginger, garlic, lemongrass and lime leaves are essential for achieving the classical flavour. An Italian salad with fresh tomatoes tastes better with fresh basil, however when making a Bolognese sauce or a stew or casserole, we would always include dried herbs such as basil, oregano, thyme and bay leaves.

These dried herbs have more robust, concentrated flavours, which amalgamate and infuse more readily into the food because they are dried, allowing the essential oils to migrate easily out of the leaf structure and flavour the meal.

Should you particularly want the flavour of some fresh herbs as well, then add them about 10 to 20 minutes before the end of cooking time. This way the heat of cooking does not destroy the delicate fresh 'top notes' and you have the best of both worlds.

So keep in mind, when it comes to fresh or dried, it is simply a matter of using the most appropriate form for the particular meal or dish.

PROCESSED HERBS

On your shopping expeditions you've probably seen the 'freshly prepared' herbs and spices in jars and tubes, which require refrigeration after opening. These are a good substitute for fresh herbs, however the flavour is sometimes sweet, salty and acidic, which is due to the amount of vinegar or other food acids needed to achieve preservation.

When using these products in cooking, taste them first and then adjust the amount of sweetness, saltiness or acidity in the dish you are making to allow for what you are adding with the prepared herbs.

the herbs

Herbs have played an important part in people's lives in many ways since time immemorial. They are renowned for their medicinal properties, their various and distinctive fragrances, their popularity with the birds and the bees and, most of all, for their unique ability to enhance the pleasure of mealtimes by contributing to the flavour of the foods we eat.

This A to Z section is a cook's guide to using, storing and growing some 50 popular culinary herbs. We also include tips on freezing and drying them, how to pick out the best and freshest bunch in the shop and recipes where the flavour of the herb is something of the hero of the event.

Some recipes are family favourites from Rosemary and John's books, others are recipes we regularly enjoy, or our daughter Kate likes to turn her hand to. And a host of generous foodie friends (old and new) including Hideo Dekura, Lucio Galleto and Timothy Fisher, Anthony Gardiner, Fiona Hammond, Lisa Lintner, Anneka Manning, Amy Nathan, Carol Selva Rajah, Charmaine Solomon and Loukie Werle have also shared recipes with us.

Some of the herbs you will read about just aren't available commercially. Take the plunge. Grow your own. Tremendous satisfaction can be achieved by growing your own herbs and the wonderful thing about them is that they can occupy as much or as little space as you like. Most herbs will grow as well in tubs and pots as they do in the garden, and a basic understanding of their requirements is all you need to grow them successfully.

angelica

angelica archangelica

With its sweet and refreshing aroma, angelica was long considered something of a guardian angel against all ills. An old-time remedy for flatulence advised chewing the stems until the condition was relieved; this was probably helpful, as we now know that angelica contains pectin, an enzyme that acts on digesting food.

Although there's a tendency to think of angelica as an old-fashioned herb, it's cultivated commercially today because it is very much in demand for medicinal and cosmetic preparations – and for the liqueur Benedictine, which wouldn't be the same without it!

Today, we are probably most familiar with angelica in its candied or crystallised form – used for decorating desserts, cakes and cassata with those brilliant green stems – and tasting overwhelmingly of sugar because of the amount you use in crystallising.

But fresh angelica stems picked straight from the plant lend a distinctive sweet flavour to jams, jellies and stewed fruits – particularly those made with tart fruits like rhubarb and plums – that's not sugary at all.

If you want fresh angelica for your cooking you will probably have to grow your own, as it is not widely available. However, once you have it in your garden, you can add a few tender leaves to salads or stock, or enhance sweet infusions by adding leaves to custard or sugar syrup. It's best to pick leaves just before you need to use them to retain the flavour. Like all herbs with juicy green leaves, chop or tear them roughly and add to hot dishes at the last minute.

You can cut and use fresh angelica stems at any time, however their flavour is usually best just after flowering.

The dried leaves make an aromatic tea and are a fragrant addition to potpourri and herb pillows. For a relaxing bath, make a simple sachet by tying a few leaves – fresh or dried – in a muslin bag and letting it soak in the hot water.

GROWING

This delicately perfumed, fast-growing plant enjoys a shady spot in the garden and needs space, taking up about as much room as a tall, fat man when it's mature – that is, 1.8 metres (6 feet) tall and 1 metre (40 in) wide. The hollow, branching stems bear a strong resemblance to celery stems, and carry bright green serrated leaves most of the year.

Angelica is a biennial, forming foliage the first summer, and round, whitish-green flower heads that bloom in late spring or early summer of the second year, when you may need to stake the plant as it gets rather top heavy. Cut the flowers (they look pretty stunning in a vase), and the leaves will grow more prolifically. And if you cut the stems back frequently, your plant may flourish for longer than the customary two years. It dies down completely in the winter but is frost-hardy.

It is best to plant seedlings or seeds in spring in a sheltered spot in the garden about 90 cm (36 in) apart. Use fresh seed, as the germinating period is very short. Angelica likes moist, well-drained, rich soil in filtered sunlight. Water well. If your plant develops yellowish-green leaves, then it's probably thirsty.

You can grow angelica in a container, but keep in mind that tall, fat man and make sure the pot is large enough to contain him and that there is enough soil to prevent him from falling flat on his face! Remember also that any plant growing in a pot is like a bird in a cage – it depends on you entirely for food and water.

DRYING

To dry the leaves, snip them off the stems and spread them out on sheets of paper or on drying racks in a shady, warm place. When they are dry and brittle, store them in an airtight container.

Harvest the seeds just before they start to fall by snipping off the flower heads and drying them. Sift out any dried husks and stalks, then store the seeds in airtight containers. If you want them for sowing, plant them within the week as angelica seeds lose their viability fast.

rosemary's glazed pears

For a spicy change, you can try a coriander seed in each pear instead of the sugar and cinnamon mixture.

4 even-sized beurre bosc pears
1 teaspoon ground cinnamon
1 teaspoon caster (superfine) sugar
butter
1 cup passionfruit pulp
4 stems candied angelica, about 2.5 cm (1 in) long

Syrup
1 cup water
½ cup caster (superfine) sugar

Wash the pears, peel and cut out the cores from the stalk end. Mix together the cinnamon and sugar. In each hollow put a knob of butter and a little of the sugar and cinnamon mixture.

Make a syrup by boiling the water and sugar together for 10 minutes. Place the pears in a saucepan, pour over the syrup, cover and simmer gently until just tender. Ladle the syrup over the pears continually so that they become nicely glazed.

Lift the pears out carefully and place them on a serving dish. Stir the passionfruit pulp into the remaining syrup to combine, then pour the mixture over the pears and decorate each one with an angelica stem. Chill, and serve with heavy cream.

Serves 4

Goat's Cheese Soufflés (recipe page 156)

Mitsuba and Tofu in Clear Soup (recipe page 111)

candied angelica

Candying angelica to decorate desserts or cakes isn't hard, but does take time.

You can reduce these amounts proportionately depending on how much stem you want to crystallise. 500 g of stem would decorate many cakes and desserts.

500 g (1 lb) fresh young stems of angelica
500 g (1 lb) caster (superfine) sugar, plus extra sugar to coat
500 ml (1 pint) water

Cut the angelica stems into 12 cm (5 in) lengths. Add enough water to cover and boil until tender. Drain and peel the stems, place them in a shallow dish and top with 500 g of sugar. Cover and set aside for two days. Transfer the stems to a saucepan, add the water and bring to the boil, stirring all the time. Reduce the heat and simmer gently until the syrup is absorbed and the stems are clear.

Place the stems on a wire rack to drain (a cake rack will do). When cool, sprinkle over plenty of sugar to coat thoroughly and leave to dry. Store the candied stems in airtight containers where they will keep well for about 6 months.

STEVIA – ANOTHER NATURALLY SWEET ALTERNATIVE

Stevia (*Stevia rebaudiana*) can, literally, be called a sweet little plant as its leaves are absolutely the sweetest product in the natural world, around 30 times sweeter than cane sugar but with no kilojoules (calories). It is increasingly used as a natural alternative to artificial sweeteners since a method was found to remove the slightly bitter aftertaste from the dried leaves.

You can use stevia leaves fresh or dried. In its dry form, less than 2 tablespoons can replace 1 cup of sugar, although it's hard to be specific as actual sweetness varies from one harvest to another.

A member of the aster family, stevia bears doily-shaped flowers in the summer. It likes fairly moist conditions and can cope with any range of temperatures above freezing. It's a rather spindly-looking plant, growing 60–90 cm (24–36 in) tall, and has pale green, narrow leaves about 2 cm (¾ in) long.

Growing stevia from seed, though possible, is a hit-and-miss operation, and therefore possibly destined to be disappointing. Taking cuttings from the mature part of the plant is a safer option. Allow them to take root in a pot of good sand or potting mixture before planting out. Sweet success.

anise

pimpinella anisum

Almost everyone will know those black, marble-sized aniseed balls that are found in specialist candy stores. Today you can even buy them over the Internet. The word aniseed is actually an abbreviation of anise seed. It is the seed of the anise plant rather than the leaf that we mostly use in cooking, which is why anise, with its warm liquorice flavour, is perhaps better known to most of us as a spice.

Originally from the Middle East, word of its usefulness as an aid to digestion (thanks to a volatile oil compound it contains called anethole) and as a breath freshener spread fast from Roman times onwards. In fact the Romans were such fans of its digestive benefits that they added aniseed to their spice-filled mustaceus cake which was served at the end of over-indulgent banquets.

Rather resembling young coriander or salad burnet, freshly picked anise leaves bring a subtle tarragon-like tang to green salads, fruit salads, soups, stews and egg dishes. Use with discretion however, so that the flavour doesn't overpower other ingredients. Add whole anise stems to vegetable soups at the start of cooking, and when the vegetables are tender, simply discard the stems as you would a bay leaf. Or, for a fresher flavour, stir through a few chopped leaves a minute or two before cooking is completed.

Whole or ground, aniseed brings distinctive liquorice and fennel notes to many traditional cuisines. The seeds are an essential ingredient in German baking and in rye breads from Scandinavia. Anise is widely used in Italian cooking, especially in puttanesca sauce with pasta and for rabbit dishes. You may also read that it's the ideal spice for Indian vegetable and seafood dishes. But the Indians more commonly choose its close cousin, fennel. The confusion arises because many people (including those who should know better, like fruit and vegetable retailers), still call the fresh fennel bulb 'aniseed', which it isn't.

Because it is a very small seed, you can use aniseed whole and simply sprinkle it over stewed or baked apples or pears, and over vegetables such as cabbages (cooked or raw), onions, cucumber, carrots, turnips and beetroot.

Anise is cultivated commercially for confectionery, cough lozenges, herb tea blends, a popular French cordial called anisette, and ouzo, pernod, pastis and aguardiente – a favourite aperitif in South America. Dogs are also rather partial to its flavour, which is just as well, because pet food manufacturers include it in pet foods as an aid to digestion and as a flatulence preventative.

Renowned for its freshness and fragrance, anise oil is an ingredient in perfumes, toothpastes, soaps and mouthwashes, and crushed aniseed is in demand for potpourri.

GROWING

A spindly plant with feathery leaves and flat, white flower heads that bloom in late summer and rise above the foliage, anise grows to about 45–50 cm (18–20 in). It likes a garden with plenty of sunshine, warmth and protection from prevailing winds. As the soft, fragile seedlings don't transplant well, sow the seeds where the plants are to grow. Make sure that the soil is well broken and in what is often called 'good seedbed condition', which basically means light and crumbly. Anise likes an alkaline soil, so you may need to add a little lime if the ground is very acid.

Plant seedlings or seeds in spring, about 30 cm (12 in) apart. Cover the seeds with a very thin layer of soil (the old rule of thumb was always that the thickness of soil cover should equal the thickness of the seed itself). Pack it down well, and keep the ground moist, using a gentle spray nozzle so that the water pressure doesn't dislodge the covering layer of soil, until the seedlings appear. Once the seeds have begun to sprout, they only have to dry out once for them to die of thirst. It is best to water anise in the late afternoon or early evening so that you do not scorch the delicate leaves.

Anise is also very happy growing in a pot, but choose one large enough for its root system and make sure it's in a sunny spot. And remember it depends on you for water.

By late summer, the flower umbels will droop with aromatic, small, brown seeds with a distinguishing fine hair at one end. The flower head is called an umbel because it's shaped in a wide, shallow dome that is almost the shape of an umbrella. Each umbel is made up of lots of very tiny individual flowers.

DRYING

Cut the heavy flower heads off before they drop, preferably before the day gets too hot, but after the dew has dried off. Spread them out to dry on sheets of paper, or tie the stems in a bunch and hang in a warm, well-ventilated area with some direct sunlight. Rub the flower heads between the palms of your hands when they are crisp and dry, then sift to separate the seeds from the flowers and pieces of stem.

Store the seeds in airtight containers away from extremes of heat, light and humidity. Try not to be impatient, because if you store the seeds before they are completely dry, you'll possibly find mould developing, and all your efforts will be wasted. Make sure you label and date the pack. Seeds will last for two to three years for culinary use, but germination is more successful if you sow seeds the following season.

puttanesca sauce

Serve with penne or your favourite pasta.

4 cloves garlic

6 anchovy fillets

$\frac{1}{2}$ teaspoon brown sugar

1 x 400 g (14 oz) can whole tomatoes

$\frac{1}{3}$ cup red wine

1 tablespoon capers

18 black olives, pitted and chopped

$\frac{1}{4}$ cup virgin olive oil

4 whole bird's eye chillies

1 tablespoon Italian herbs

$\frac{1}{2}$ teaspoon aniseed

Make a paste by crushing the garlic cloves with the anchovies in a pestle and mortar. Combine the paste with all the other ingredients in a pan and simmer gently for 30 minutes, uncovered, until the sauce has reduced and the flavours have blended and developed.

Serves 4

compôte of dates with figs and aniseed

Serve a small amount of this delicious compôte with cream, or enjoy with cheese, crackers and fruit.

1 cup pitted dates, halved or quartered

1 cup tenderised dried figs, cut to similar size as the dates

1 cup port

1 teaspoon aniseed

To make the compôte, place all the ingredients in a small pan and bring to the boil, then remove immediately from heat and cover. Let the compôte cool to room temperature before lifting the lid off the pan. By this time, most of the liquid should be absorbed. Store in the refrigerator until needed.

Makes about 2 cups

balm

melissa officinalis

The lingering lemon-scent of this member of the mint family gave it the popular name of lemon balm. Also called heart's delight and the elixir of life, balm was long highly regarded as a remedy to revive the spirits. It was traditionally used in pickled herrings and eels in Belgium and Holland, the lemon overtones complementing the seafood. It was also used in liqueurs such as chartreuse. These days balm is considered rather old-fashioned and is sought after more for its cottage-garden appeal than its culinary use.

But balm's palate-pleasing, lemon-flavoured leaves deliver a distinctive tang to a green salad with a light-on-vinegar dressing or to lightly steamed vegetables. Try adding a few bruised leaves to fresh fruit salad or a compôte of oranges – or use as a substitute for mint for a refreshing change. Season chicken, fish or pork with a little finely chopped balm before serving. It's traditional to add fresh sprigs to wine cups and fruit drinks, while chopped leaves are added to fruit salads, stewed fruit and fruit jellies. Infuse a sprig in custard, removing it just before you serve so that only the lemon fragrance lingers.

Balm tea is refreshing; even one leaf in the teapot with Indian tea will give a lift. The dried leaves make a fragrant addition to potpourri and herb pillows.

A small bunch, washed, wrapped in foil and stored in the refrigerator will stay fresh for a week or two. Another option is to stand the bunch in a jar of water and cover it entirely with a plastic bag, folding the open ends under the base of the jar. To keep longer than a week, chop fresh leaves finely into ice-cube trays, cover with a little water and freeze.

GROWING

Balm, a compact leafy plant with crinkly leaves similar to mint, grows to about 60–75 cm (24–30 in) depending on conditions. It likes a sunny garden with moist, rich soil. Sow the seeds in spring fairly thickly, or plant seedlings close together and you will soon find you have a pleasing clump. When buying seeds or seedlings, opt for a frost-hardy variety. From late spring, out shoot long thin flower stalks covered with clusters of tiny, white, bee-attracting blooms.

This perennial has something of a spreading habit, but its thick, matted, shallow roots are not as rampant as mint. Cut it back quite hard in late autumn, and you will see plenty of new growth coming up by spring. Fungus can be a problem if conditions are too wet and shady, and keep a watch out for voracious leaf-eating grubs and insects.

The simplest way to propagate balm is by root division in spring, just as the new growth is starting. To take cuttings, wait for new tips to grow to about 7.5 cm (3 in) long, and when firm enough, take a 10 cm (4 in) long tip, removing all the leaves except the top two. Press the cuttings deeply into a pot of river sand or good quality potting mix, leaving one-third of each cutting exposed.

If you are growing balm in a pot, choose one with plenty of room for its shallow, rampant root system. And remember to water regularly because, as with all shallow-rooted plants, as soon as the top layer of soil is dry, balm gets thirsty.

DRYING

Because balm's delicate lemon fragrance is easily destroyed on drying, fresh is best. If you really want to dry the leaves, cut the stalks back almost to ground level just as the flowers begin to appear and dry them on airy racks in a shady place. You can also tie them loosely together in bunches and hang them to dry. As soon as the leaves are crisp and dry, cut them from their stalks and store in airtight, labelled containers.

chicken salad with lemon balm and thai spices

Balm's palate-pleasing, lemon-flavoured leaves deliver a distinctive tang to this chicken salad.

500 g (1 lb) chicken tenderloins
1 teaspoon sesame oil
1 teaspoon thick soy sauce
3 cups baby rocket leaves
1 cup lemon balm leaves, loosely packed
1 cup coriander leaves, loosely packed

Dressing
¼ cup lime juice
2 tablespoons sesame oil
1 tablespoon fish sauce
2 tablespoons mirin or sherry
2 small red chillies, finely sliced
2 teaspoons gula melaka or brown sugar
1 clove garlic, crushed

Preheat the oven to 200ºC (400ºF). Mix the oil and soy sauce together and brush over the chicken pieces. Place them on an oiled baking tray and bake for about 15 minutes, or until cooked, turning once. Remove from the oven and set aside.

To make the dressing, combine all the ingredients in a jar and shake well. Place the rocket, lemon balm and coriander on serving plates, top with the chicken, and spoon dressing over.

Serves 4

swiss breakfast

65 g (2½ oz) rolled oats (not the instant ones)
200 g (7 oz) plain yoghurt
juice of 1 orange
1 apple (skin left on), diced
2 tablespoons raisins
2 teaspoons chopped balm
2 teaspoons finely chopped walnuts
raw sugar or honey, to taste

Combine all the ingredients in a bowl and serve with extra raw sugar or honey to taste.

Serves 1

BALM FOR BEES

Herb gardens and bee hives were traditionally linked together, and Thomas Hyll wrote in 1579 that the hives should be placed near: 'The hearbe Baulme ... and manye other sweete and wholesome floures.' Balm's association with bees goes back over 2,000 years when every pantry was packed with jars of honey and hives were traditionally rubbed with sweet-smelling herbs, especially balm leaves, to prevent the bees from swarming and to encourage them to come home.

basil

SWEET BASIL *ocimum basilicum*

BUSH BASIL *ocimum minimum*

Versatile sweet basil with its heady, clove-and-anise perfume sends cooks into raptures and brings summer to mind. As the taste of the fresh leaves is less pungent than the aroma, you can safely use a whole bunch in your cooking if you are so inclined. However, in its fresh state, it has quite a peppery pungency, so be judicious if you still want other flavours to shine through.

Basil has a special affinity with tomatoes and tomato-based dishes and is excellent with eggplant (aubergine), zucchini (courgette), marrow, squash, and spinach. Added during the last 30 minutes of cooking, basil brings zest to split pea, bean or lentil soups. It is delicious with cream or cottage cheese in sandwiches, lifts crisp green salads and enhances pasta dishes. Above all, it gives pesto its unique character. Basil also complements poultry, veal, fish and shellfish and its volatile notes counteract the richness of liver and game in pâtés and terrines. In fact, as any true 'basilophile' will tell you, it can be added to just about anything! Simply steep a few fresh, washed leaves in a bottle of white wine vinegar for a few weeks and you will have tasty vinegar on hand for dressings.

Basil leaves are best when used whole or torn. Chefs say that you shouldn't cut them with a knife because this takes away some of their aroma.

When buying basil, steer clear of bunches that have black marks on the leaves or look wilted. Fresh basil will keep in the refrigerator for a couple of weeks. Simply wrap paper towelling around the base of the stems, wet it and seal the whole bunch in a plastic bag. Leaves can be frozen too: tear them finely, mix with a little water and freeze in ice-cube trays.

To preserve basil in oil or vinegar, pick the leaves, wash and dry them and stack in a shallow container, sprinkling salt on each leaf as you go. Cover the leaves in olive oil, pop the lid on the container and store in the refrigerator for up to three months.

Varieties of basil have long been important in South-East Asian cooking – Thai cookery uses three main kinds. Probably the best known is Thai basil *(O. canum sims)* with its slender, oval, slightly hairy leaves. The leaves are eaten raw with vermicelli, chopped and served as a garnish on fish curries, added to salads or included in clear vegetable soups. The seeds, known as *subja*, swell and become gelatinous in water and are used in desserts and drinks.

GROWING

The old favourites, sweet basil and bush basil, with their tender bright green leaves, are still the best varieties to grow for the kitchen. Sweet basil is the most popular and is a vigorous grower in the summer months. For limited space, bush basil is more compact but with the same wonderful flavour. Both produce small, white, long-stamened flowers that you have to nip in the bud ruthlessly to prevent the plants from going to seed and finishing the life cycle too soon. Nipping also encourages thicker foliage and thus more basil, a more abundant harvest and more pesto …

This easy-to-grow, sun-loving annual thrives on heat and turns up its toes with the first wintry blasts. If your soil is sour, lime it well two weeks before planting, making sure that the bed is well broken up and as fine as possible. If the soil is heavy, a small quantity of river sand will help to make the ground more suitable, both for sowing and drainage. Plant seedlings or sow seeds directly into the garden in late spring or early summer when the weather is definitely warm as a cold change can kill the plants. Thin out sweet basil seedlings to 30 cm (12 in) between plants. For bush basil, 15 cm (6 in) between seedlings is plenty. Pinch out the centres to encourage branching and a sturdy, spreading, bushy habit.

Water well and keep moist (but don't drown) to ensure germination and good growth and remember that snails are very partial to young basil leaves and can devour a seedling at a single sitting. If your young plants develop horrible black spots on the leaves, it could be from water staying on the leaves overnight. To prevent this, only water the plants in the morning once they are established, and bring a pot under cover in the event of wet weather.

Pick fresh leaves throughout the summer and harvest in the early autumn before the cold weather turns the leaves limp and yellow. In hot climates where basil can grow throughout the year, the seeds will often self-sow.

Basil makes a pretty border as the plants sit so neatly in the garden. The more compact bush basil is a good choice for balcony baskets and pots. Choose an 18 cm (7 in) pot; fill it with a good quality potting mix and plant three or four seedlings. When they are established, leave the sturdiest in the pot, pick out the rest and plant them in other containers or in the garden. Remember that basil (or any other herb) is not a houseplant. It wants a warm terrace or exterior windowsill where there is sunshine and fresh air. A lack of both of these elements could lead to black, rotting stems and a very sick plant.

DRYING

For the fullest flavour, cut long, leafy stalks for drying, and spread them out in a shady place on wire mesh to encourage quick drying. Do not hang them in bunches, as the soft foliage will dry too slowly and may possibly spoil. Oven or microwave drying is not satisfactory as the leaves bruise easily and are liable to scorch.

perfect pesto

There's no need to introduce pesto. If you work your way through our 'dollop' suggestions on page 20, you'll soon need to whip up another batch.

4 packed cups basil leaves
8 cloves garlic
1 cup toasted pine nuts
1 cup good quality parmesan cheese, finely grated
1 cup extra virgin olive oil
salt and pepper, to taste

Combine ingredients in a food processor adding a little of each at a time. Stop to stir once or twice. Will store in the refrigerator for up to 3 weeks.

Makes 2 cups

basil variations

This delicious 'variation' recipe is reproduced with kind permission from Amy Nathan, from her book *Openers*, (Chronicle Books, San Francisco, 1988).

2 tablespoons vinegar

salt to taste

4 small fresh eggs

500 g (1 lb) yellow wax beans,
   ends trimmed and cut lengthwise into strips

1 handful each green and opal basil leaves, mixed

¼ cup light olive oil

3 tablespoons white wine vinegar

3 bacon slices, cooked and crumbled

cracked black pepper

8 thin baguette slices, toasted lightly

1 cup Perfect Pesto (see page 19)

In a pan, bring 5 cm (2 in) depth of water to a gentle boil. Add the vinegar and salt, and poach the eggs in the liquid. As yolks begin to set (about 5 minutes), transfer the eggs with a slotted spatula to a shallow pan of cool water to hold for serving.

Blanch or steam the beans for approximately 2 minutes, or until tender. Rinse under cold water and set aside. Cut half the basil leaves into thin strips and set aside, reserving some whole leaves for garnish. In a large bowl, combine the olive oil and vinegar. Toss the beans in enough dressing to coat.

Divide the beans among 4 serving plates. Sprinkle each serving with basil strips and a little bacon. Top with one poached egg, being sure to allow excess water to run off eggs before placing over the beans. Sprinkle with cracked pepper and add some whole basil leaves to each plate. Serve with baguette toasts spread with Perfect Pesto.

Serves 4 as an entrée

add a dollop of pesto to:

- a bowl of minestrone
- a crusty roll
- a bowl of pasta
- cheese and crackers
- salad dressings
- oven-dried tomatoes
- grilled chicken slices
- stuffings
- goat's cheese canapés
- rare roast beef

WHAT YOU NEED TO KNOW WHEN CHOOSING BASIL PLANTS

With the immense popularity of this herb, nurserymen have had a field day producing new and fascinating varieties, such as lemon, purple, pesto, lime, ruffled, and dark opal basils.

CAMPHOR BASIL – *Ocimum kilimansharicum*
– an interesting variety, but not suitable for eating.

CINNAMON BASIL – *O. basilicum 'cinnamon'*
– for novelty value, try a few leaves in fruit salad. Dry and add to potpourri.

GREEN RUFFLES BASIL – *O. basilicum 'green ruffles'*
– simply gorgeous in salads.

LEMON BASIL 'SWEET DANI' – *O. sp.*
– a delightful blend of flavours. Toss some shredded leaves in a chicken salad.

LIME BASIL – *O. americanum*
– add whole leaves to cool drinks, or place a few leaves on fish before wrapping in foil to barbecue.

PERENNIAL BASIL – *O. sp.*
– has the benefit of lasting through the winter, but the flavour is not as good as sweet basil. Enjoy the seasonality that nature intended – basil is a summer flavour.

PURPLE RUFFLES BASIL – *O. basilicum 'purple ruffles'*
– showy in the garden. Great in salads.

RED RUBIN BASIL – *O. basilicum 'red rubin'*
– another showy-in-the-garden and great-in-salads variety.

SACRED BASIL – *O. sanctum*
– this faintly lemon-scented basil has a warm aniseed aroma and a pretty mauve-pink flower. Many a Hindu home will have a pot growing by the front door. Do likewise and choose a more appropriate variety for your meals.

THAI BASIL *O. basilicum 'anise'*
– quite different from sweet basil. Absolutely essential for authentic Thai cooking.
Note: Japanese basil is in fact a herb called shiso and is not related to European basil.

bay tree

lauris nobilis

The bay tree is a fairly unremarkable evergreen tree. If you saw it in an old, well-established garden, you'd probably not notice it amongst the rhododendrons and more showy specimens. But an avenue of bays can be quite stunning in its simplicity. The long, narrow, dark green leaves have a dull gloss, giving a healthy tree a rather radiant look. And when you break or crush the leaves, the volatile oils give off a warmly pungent aroma with fresh camphor notes; younger leaves are lighter and less aromatic.

Mediterranean and Middle Eastern soups and stews, and traditional roasts just wouldn't be the same without bay's lingering, pungent flavour. Add one or two dried leaves (too much spoils the flavour) to fish, meat and poultry recipes that need long, slow cooking. Bay also has an affinity with vegetable and pasta dishes, and especially with tomatoes.

Parsimony pays when cooking with bay because the strong flavour amalgamates readily during cooking but all too easily overpowers. Bay combines well with basil, garlic, oregano, paprika, pepper, rosemary and sage and makes an appearance in *herbes de Provence* mixes and in pickling spices.

Dried bay leaves are better than fresh for cooking. Look for clean, dark green ones – the darker the better. Yellow leaves are poor quality and may have been exposed to light for too long. Powdered bay leaves are convenient, but buy small quantities as they lose their flavour within 12 months of grinding.

GROWING

Bay trees can grow to about 10 metres (33 feet). Trimmed into tidy balls of foliage on slender stems, the trees look very elegant in doorway tubs – those potted toffee-apple trees bracketing restaurant and corporate doorways in many American movies of the 1960s are usually bay trees. They can also be grown as a hedge, as left to themselves they send up many suckers. Although they do best with good quality, well-drained soil, they actually come from the rocky, parched hillsides of the Mediterranean, so they are quite hardy. Bay trees are fairly slow growers, but they do shoot up if they have to compete with taller plants for the sunshine.

Propagation is best from cuttings, as there's about a 95 per cent failure rate in trying to germinate their pea-sized, nut-hard seeds. Take 15 cm (6 in) long cuttings of new wood when the fresh spring leaves have just hardened. Break the cutting away from the old wood, leaving a 6 mm (¼ in) heel. Trim the heel carefully with a sharp knife to remove any overhanging bark. Strip the bottom leaves off the cutting, leaving about two-thirds of the stalk bare to insert into a pot of river sand or a good quality potting mix (choose one with good water retention qualities). Just firm the cuttings down with your fingers and keep them watered. By the end of spring they should have made roots and be ready to plant out. Pots are best (for the first year at least) for slow growers like bay.

Bay blooms mid- to late-spring. The waxy cream flowers, though small, are intensely scented, nectar-filled, and much loved by bees. The flowers are followed by purple berries that have no culinary use at all. Don't be tempted to experiment – they contain laurostearine and lauric acid and are poisonous.

Bay is very susceptible to white wax scale which affects leaf growth and makes the leaves sooty and unattractive, to say the least. You can control it by spraying with white oil in hot weather or scrubbing the affected places with soapy water. A word to the wise – act as soon as you see the scale appearing, because once it reaches epidemic proportions, you'll have a hard time scrubbing the whole tree!

DRYING

If you have your own bay tree, you can pick mature, dark, firm leaves for drying year-round. Try to take only the stalks that are at least a year old. Never pick the most recent growth for drying. To dry leaves (and stop them from curling), cut them off the stem and spread them out in a single layer over a piece of gauze on a wire rack or insect screen. Cover with more gauze, weight with small pieces of wood to keep flat and leave to dry somewhere that's dark and well aired for about five days. Alternatively, hang leafy branches in bunches to dry. Remove the leaves from the stems when they are crisp-dry and store them in airtight containers in a cool cupboard away from light so that they will keep their colour and quality (for up to three years).

tuna and fresh fennel stew

We've adapted this recipe from one of Loukie Werle's, from her book, *The Trattoria Table* (Webber & Werle Publishing, 1994). Our version for the 'fennelophile' uses less tuna and much more fennel.

2 bulbs fennel, thinly sliced

1 onion, chopped

2 cloves garlic, finely chopped

2 tablespoons extra virgin olive oil

1 x 400 g (14 oz) can whole tomatoes

2 dried bay leaves

¼ cup continental parsley

1 generous strip lemon rind

2 tablespoons freshly squeezed lemon juice

½ cup white wine

500 g (1 lb) fresh tuna, cut into bite-sized cubes

1 cup fish stock

salt and freshly ground black pepper

¼ cup chopped fennel leaves

Combine the fennel, onion, garlic and oil in a large pan and cook over moderate heat, stirring frequently until just softened, about 5 minutes. Add the tomatoes and cook for a further 5 minutes, stirring frequently. Add the bay leaves, parsley, lemon rind and juice and the wine and simmer for about 20 minutes. Just before serving, add the tuna and simmer until cooked, about 3–4 minutes.

Transfer the tuna and vegetables to a bowl with a slotted spoon and reduce the liquid by about a third. Discard the bay leaves and lemon rind and return the tuna and vegetables to the pan. Heat through, seasoning to taste with salt and pepper. Sprinkle over the fennel leaves and serve the stew with plenty of crusty bread to mop up the sensational juices.

Serves 4

Gyoza with Kaffir Lime Leaf (recipe page 85)

Watercress Sandwiches (recipe page 55)

bay leaf sorbet

This aromatic sorbet is reproduced with very kind permission from *Herbes de Provence* by Anthony Gardiner (New Holland, 2002).

200 g (7 oz) caster (superfine) sugar
juice of 1 lemon
2 cups water
4 dried bay leaves, plus extra for garnish

Combine the sugar, lemon juice and water in a saucepan. Bring to the boil, then add the bay leaves. Remove from the heat, cover with a lid and leave to infuse for at least 30 minutes. Lift out the bay leaves, and churn the mixture in an ice-cream maker for 30 minutes.

If you don't have an ice-cream machine, pour the sorbet mixture into a metal tray or bowl and freeze. Stir after about an hour, and then every half an hour after that so that the ice crystals are broken down into small particles as they form. Four stirrings should be enough.

Remove the sorbet from the freezer 10–15 minutes before serving, and decorate each serving with a fresh bay leaf.

Serves 4

bouquet garni

Bay leaves are an essential ingredient in *bouquet garni* – a savoury posy or bunch of herbs – where they are firmly tied together with sprigs of parsley, marjoram and thyme; sometimes a few peppercorns and a stalk of celery are added.

Drop the *bouquet garni* into the pot at the beginning of cooking then remove it just before serving (the herbs can look rather drab and worn when they have done their job).

When a *bouquet garni* is made using dried herbs, they can be crushed and stirred directly into the pot; however, traditionalists like to tie up the dried herbs in muslin, so they can easily be lifted out just before serving.

INDIAN BAY LEAVES

If you come across a reference to Indian bay leaves or *tejpat* in an Indian cookery book, what the writer is talking about is cinnamon leaves. The evergreen cinnamon tree is a beautiful addition to any garden in tropical or temperate areas. It's a member of the laurel family, which includes the bay laurel and the avocado. Its aromatic leaves, just like the twigs and bark, have their uses. Young cinnamon leaves are an intense red, maturing to a dark glossy green with conspicuous white veins running lengthwise down the leaf. They have a distinctive clove-like aroma and flavour, and are used fresh or dried, in Indian and Asian cooking in curries and slow-cooked pot meals. If you have a tree, select mature leaves, preferably last year's growth, snip them with secateurs and use them fresh in your cooking.

bergamot

monarda didyma

LEMON BERGAMOT *monarda citriodora*

Bergamot is the show-off of the herb garden. Its spidery, shaggy, pompom blooms in pinks, mauves and rich reds dominate the herb garden greens in early summer. The bees are in a frenzy of delight over this fragrant orange-scented, nectar-packed plant, so it's no wonder it is sometimes known as 'bee balm'. Honey-eating birds like it too. Bergamot is known in North America as Oswego Tea because the Oswego Indians used the leaves as an infusion.

The slightly hairy leaves are best fresh in tossed salads, fruit jellies, teas and cool summery drinks, delivering a flavour reminiscent of thyme, sage and rosemary. Bergamot also combines well with vegetables, duck, pork and veal dishes.

The leaves make a fragrant change from mint or basil, and the soft honeyed flowers can be gently torn and added to salads. 'Cambridge Scarlet' is the best known of the red bergamots and is the variety most often used in cooking. Pink flowering bergamot with its lemon, pepper and thyme-flavoured leaves complements meat dishes.

If you want fresh bergamot, you'll probably have to grow your own as fruit and vegetable retailers are unlikely to stock it. This is another of those 'best fresh' herbs. But you can stock up on fresh supplies year round if you freeze finely chopped leaves mixed with a little water in ice-cube trays. Or, carefully place fresh flowers in an ice-cube tray, gently cover with water and freeze.

The dried flowers and leaves make a fragrant addition to potpourri and a revitalising hot bath.

The oil of bergamot that is famous for flavouring Earl Grey tea doesn't come from this herb at all. It comes from a citrus fruit, bergamot orange (*Citrus bergamia*). In fact the herb was named after the orange because the aromas are so similar.

GROWING

Position! Position! Position! Bergamot needs the right spot. Its creeping, matted root system wants to be cool and moist, but the leaves and flowers like to bask in the morning sun for an hour or two. Bergamot grows to 1.2 metres (4 feet), making it ideal for shady background clumps in the herb garden or decorative clusters in the flowerbed. In the right position, the tubular red flowers bloom from early summer right through to autumn on their 90 cm (36 in) stalks. At Somerset Cottage, there was a distant bed of bergamot set in the lawn and surrounded by leafy trees. In summer, not one member of the Hemphill family could resist its splashes of vivid red, and would often rush down to pick a flower or sip a honey-laden petal.

Plant seeds or seedlings in spring in rich, moist soil about 15 cm (6 in) apart. And prepare for snails, because they are more than partial to the irresistible combination of shady moist conditions and soft young bergamot leaves. Stake the slender, rather brittle stems that shoot up in summer and mulch during hot weather. After flowering has finished, cut this perennial back to ground level. Propagate by root division year round.

DRYING

Harvest the leaves and flowers in late summer when the plant is in full bloom and dry as quickly as possible. Pick the leaves and blooms off the stems and spread them out on a wire rack or insect screen in a shady, airy place. As always, when drying, the words to remember are 'dark' and 'dry'. When the leaves and flowers are crisp-dry, store in airtight containers.

tomato and bergamot loaf

Serve this Hemphill family favourite from Somerset Cottage days straight from the oven with a mesclun and fresh herb salad on the side.

1½ cups canned tomatoes with liquid

2 tablespoons water or tomato juice

2 tablespoons chopped fresh bergamot leaves

½ cup lightly roasted pine nuts

½ cup finely chopped celery

1 cup grated tasty cheese

2 tablespoons virgin olive oil

1 small onion, roughly grated

1 teaspoon each salt and paprika

2 eggs, beaten

Preheat the oven to 180°C (350°F). Break up the tomatoes and combine with the remaining ingredients. Spoon the mixture into an oiled ovenproof dish and bake for 20 minutes.

Serves 4

borage

borago officinalis

The whiskered leaves of borage have a faint cucumber flavour, and its leaves and flowers impart this fresh aroma to cool drinks. You must use the very young leaves, otherwise the gentle whiskers are more like two-day-old stubble! Chop them very finely and mix with cottage cheese or cream cheese, and use the mixture in sandwiches and salads. The young leaves are delicious cooked in tempura batter and served Japanese-style, and the leaves and flowers are used for herbal teas. In making our Borage Soup, it is quite amazing how the cooked borage and potatoes smell like Jerusalem artichokes.

As borage is rich in mineral salts such as potassium and calcium, the finely chopped leaves make a useful seasoning in a low-sodium diet.

Borage flowers are literally the stars of the edible-flower world. The five-pointed stars of pure blue petals are ideal for crystallising to decorate cakes and desserts, and the clusters of demurely drooping flowers have long been favourite subjects for painters, ceramic artists and embroiderers. Bees love the nectar-rich blossoms, which were once floated in the stirrup cups given to the Crusaders and to the gladiators in Roman times – perhaps this was because they were traditionally thought to give courage.

Borage leaves and flowers are generally used fresh. Your best option is to grow your own if you want to enjoy this popular, self-sowing, culinary herb year round because the plant wilts so quickly after picking, making it nigh on impossible to find good quality leaves to buy.

The flowers freeze well. Pick them when they are just fully opened and freeze whole by carefully putting them one by one in an ice-cube tray and gently covering them with water. When you want to impress your guests with your panache and originality, a flowery ice-block can be dropped into a glass of fruit juice, gin and tonic, or any other beverage.

GROWING

Borage grows to 1 metre (40 in) high and about 75 cm (30 in) wide and has a thick, hollow central stalk. Because the stalk is hollow, it's not very strong, and as the plant grows, it needs a stake to help bear the weight, otherwise your borage plant will fall about all over your garden.

The stalk and the branching stems are covered with stubbly hairs. The broad fleshy leaves are hairy too, becoming pricklier as they mature, and the clustered buds are covered in a soft down. The leaves when fully grown are approximately 23 cm (9 in) long and 15 cm (6 in) wide. The flowers are star-shaped and a pure blue, with an occasional pale pink bloom appearing amongst the blue. There is also a rare variety with white flowers.

Borage will bloom nearly all through the year, and is continually seeding itself, so once planted, you should never be without it. It seems to do best when allowed to grow in thick clumps; the plants help to support each other and the massed effect of the downy buds and blue flowers is quite delightful. If, on the other hand, borage begins to take over the garden, it is easily thinned out and the shallow roots dislodged – even when fully grown – by pulling out the stems by hand, remembering that the stalks are prickly.

Gourmet snails find young borage plants very tempting, so be sure to protect them either with snail bait or a 'magic circle' of coiled rope or sand. Snails can't navigate these barriers. Established plants can be susceptible to a rather unsightly form of mildew, usually late in the season. At this stage it is probably better to dig the plant up and dispose of it rather than resort to chemicals.

Borage is easily grown in any light, moist, well-drained, rich soil. It is a hardy annual and continually self-sows, thriving just as well in winter in temperate zones as it does in summer. Once the plant is established it usually looks after itself and will keep coming up, often in unexpected places.

Borage seed germinates so easily that it can be sown year round in mild climates. In very cold areas, the best time for planting is in spring, when the oblong black seeds can be sown directly into the garden about 30 cm (12 in) apart. Make sure that the ground has been well turned over first, so that the soil is reasonably fine. Borage likes a sunny position that is sheltered from the wind as the soft main stems are easily broken – another reason for giving it a stake for support.

Borage is quite happy in a tub, but make sure there's plenty of room for its root system and has a stake to prop it up, and remember you will need to fertilise.

DRYING

If you're really keen to try it, drying the leaves and flowers is possible, but it's hardly necessary with such a prolific plant. You have to be quick to prevent spoilage as the leaves wilt so quickly after picking. Pick unblemished leaves and opened flowers after the dew has gone. Take the flowers and leaves off the succulent stalks and place them on wire racks in a shady, airy place. When dry and brittle, store them separately in airtight containers.

borage soup

For that extra special touch, top each bowl of this creamy soup with a fresh borage flower before serving.

2 large potatoes, peeled and cubed
2 cups vegetable stock
a good handful young borage leaves, washed and chopped
    (about 1 cup)
150 ml (5 fl oz) pouring cream
$\frac{1}{2}$ teaspoon grated nutmeg
borage flowers, allow 1 per serving

Simmer the potatoes in the stock until almost tender. Add the borage leaves and continue cooking for a few minutes further until the potato is cooked. Let the soup cool a little before blending in batches in the food processor until smooth. Return the soup to the saucepan, add cream and nutmeg, and reheat before serving. Garnish each serving with a borage flower.

Serves 2

borage tempura

To make borage tempura, you need to rinse the leaves and dry them well first. Don't worry about the little whiskers, they will not be noticeable once they are cooked.

20 young borage leaves
120 g ($4\frac{1}{2}$ oz) cornflour (cornstarch) or potato flour
120 g ($4\frac{1}{2}$ oz) plain (all-purpose) flour
400 ml (14 fl oz) very cold water
vegetable oil for deep-frying

Make the batter by combining the flours and cold water in a bowl and whisking until well blended. Heat the oil in a deep saucepan or deep-fryer until a blob of batter dropped in sizzles and cooks immediately.

Dip each leaf in the batter, allowing excess batter to drain off, then deep-fry until crisp and golden brown, around 50 seconds. Spread the fried leaves out on kitchen paper to absorb excess oil.

Serves 1–2

caraway

carum carvi

Imagine a family sitting around their cave some five thousand years ago enjoying an evening meal with the distinctive flavour of caraway. Not a culinary 'Hobbit' fantasy at all. Caraway has long been valued as both a spice and herb for its culinary and digestive benefits and traces of this native of Europe and western Asia have even been found in remains of meals dating back to the Mesolithic era.

With its warm, fresh fennel and anise notes, caraway seems to be something of an acquired taste; and not one that's always popular with children. But its culinary versatility is unquestioned, and it is found in breads and cakes throughout Europe – rye bread and caraway seed cake perhaps being the best known. In Germany, Scandinavia and the Balkan countries it's a familiar flavouring in soups and stews, with cabbage and potato dishes, sprinkled over root vegetables and added to breads and cheese. Caraway is also a key ingredient in Tunisia's fiery harissa paste and in the best blends of India's garam masala, where its pungency is cleverly blended with other spices so that it is not overpowering.

It's easy to make the most of these versatile seeds. Simply shake a few over apples, quinces and pears when baking or stewing. Sprinkle over turnips, beetroot, parsnips, carrots, cabbage and cauliflower during cooking and add to potato and onion gratin dishes. Blend into cream cheese. Combine with home-made breads, biscuits and cakes. If you find the flavour of the whole seeds a little strong, as it can be for the uninitiated, grind some seeds in a mortar and pestle, mix with a little salt and pepper, and use in any of the ways just mentioned. Remember that discretion is sometimes the better part of valour!

If you want freshly picked young leaves for salads and soups in spring and early summer, you will have to grow your own. Add the leaves, whole or finely chopped, to spring soups in the last 20 or 30 minutes cooking time. They also give a spicy tang to green salads and add flavour to green vegetables such as spinach and zucchini (courgette).

Caraway's thick and tapering roots look rather like small parsnips or carrots and they can be sliced, steamed and eaten in much the same way. Be adventurous and try them with a little melted butter. If you discover that you are rather partial to caraway cooked this way, it may be worthwhile sowing two crops – one for the root (you pull the roots when the plant is still young) and the other for the seeds. That will ensure there are always plenty of delicate leaves to add to salads and soups.

The oil expressed from the seeds is an ingredient in gin, schnapps, kummel and aquavit and flavours chewing gums, mouthwashes and toothpastes.

Because caraway was said to prevent lovers from straying, it was considered to be an essential ingredient in love potions. Perhaps this is why the seed, baked in dough, is often placed in the cote to make sure the pigeons come home.

GROWING

This delicate plant with lacy, frond-like foliage, has summer-blooming flowers that appear in the second year. The flowers themselves are so tiny that the flower umbel almost looks like the skeleton of a flower head even when in full bloom. When the flowers die, they are followed by fruit or capsules that explode when ripe, scattering the dark brown, crescent-shaped, aromatic, versatile seeds.

This self-seeding annual can grow to 60 cm (24 in) in a sunny, sheltered position in the garden. If you want to grow caraway, take yourself off to the local nursery and buy seedlings, as the germination failure rate is very high with seeds. Plant seedlings in late spring in medium-textured, well-drained soil about 20 cm (8 in) apart. Fertilise for best results. If you are determined to start from scratch, sow seeds in early spring in the garden, again about 20 cm (8 in) apart. Caraway seedlings do not like being moved, so there's no need to start them in seed boxes. However, they are perfectly happy in a pot as long as it's in a sunny, sheltered spot, but please remember to provide water. And to fertilise. Whether in a pot or garden bed, caraway's decorative tiny white flowers tend to attract beneficial insects.

This is one plant that you want to go to seed. Let the minute, white, umbrella-like flower heads fade and the petals fall, so that the tiny aromatic fruit or capsules that hold the seeds will form.

DRYING

In autumn, cut the heavy flower heads off before they drop. Caraway needs to be harvested in the very early morning while the dew is still condensed on the fragile umbels; once dry, the seeds will scatter all over the garden as you try to collect them.

Spread the flowers out to dry on sheets of paper in a warm, well-ventilated area with some direct sunlight. The seeds are ready to store when the fruit falls away easily from the shrivelled flower heads if given a light shake. Sieve out any pieces of stalk and pack the seeds into airtight containers.

root vegetable tagine

Finely slice the vegetables into rounds and serve this tangy tagine over couscous.

1 tablespoon mild paprika

1 tablespoon ground coriander seed

1 teaspoon cinnamon

salt and pepper to taste

1 or 2 caraway roots, peeled and sliced

1 swede or turnip, peeled and sliced

2 parsnips, peeled and sliced

3 carrots, peeled and sliced

1 tablespoon virgin oil

1 x 400 g (14 oz) can tomatoes

2 cups vegetable stock

Combine the spices with the salt and pepper and toss through the root vegetables. Heat the oil in a heavy-based pan or casserole, add the root vegetables and cook gently for 5 minutes. Add the tomatoes and enough stock to cover, stir, then cover with a lid and simmer for 30 minutes or until the vegetables are tender (this will depend on how finely you have sliced them).

Serves 4

chamomile

ENGLISH CHAMOMILE *chamaemelum nobile (syn. anthemis nobilis)*

GERMAN CHAMOMILE *matriccaria recutita*

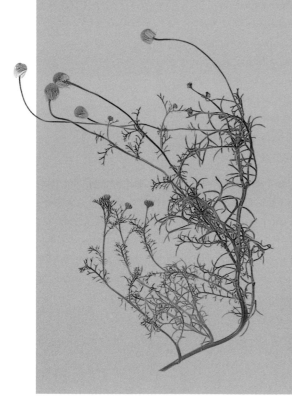

This is the herb loved by natural blondes! Chamomile tea is famous not only as a calming cuppa, but as a super highlighting rinse for fair hair – numerous shampoos proudly (and loudly) proclaim their chamomile content.

Perennial English (also known as Roman) chamomile is a great addition to herb and cottage gardens, with its low-growing, spreading ferny foliage and yellow-centred, white-petalled flowers like tiny daisies on long thin stems. The Spanish called this chamomile *manzanilla* (little apple) because of the apple aroma of the leaves. Although both the flowers and foliage are edible, chamomile flowers are used almost exclusively for making tea or for infusions for cosmetic use.

German chamomile is an annual with a more upright stance and a wonderful profusion of flowers during the summer. It is widely used in natural therapies as its highly scented dried flower heads contain an aromatic oil that has powerful antiseptic and anti-inflammatory properties.

If anyone tells you they have a yellow-petalled chamomile, they are probably referring to a daisy-like plant known as Dyer's chamomile, which should not be used as an alternative to true chamomile.

Chamomile is an excellent addition to the compost heap, so put spent chamomile tea flowers there, and even your old chamomile tea bags, as well as any unwanted foliage or plants.

GROWING

The spreading perennial English and annual German varieties are by far the most popular chamomiles to grow.

English chamomile (possibly called 'chamomile flowering lawn' in your local plant nursery or garden shop) has fine, feathery leaves and a creeping, matting habit, which makes a beautiful, if somewhat tousled, informal lawn. For good coverage, you'll need a minimum of about 30 plants per square metre (25 plants per square yard) and pre-ordered 'plugs' are available. In a dry season chamomile needs to be kept well watered, but it will reward you in late summer when it sends up stems of flower heads to about 30 cm (12 in). Cut the flowers to dry for herb tea, and then run the mower over the lawn with the blades set fairly high.

German chamomile thrives in a sunny, well-drained spot. It grows quickly into a bushy little plant about 45–60 cm (18–24 in) high that has fine foliage and bears flowers profusely for quite some time throughout the warmer months.

Plant seedlings or propagate English chamomile by root division. Sow German chamomile seeds in spring. Work the soil very well before planting if it is heavy, add some sandy loam, dampen the ground, and put in the divided roots or seeds.

As the seeds are very small, you may prefer to start them off in a prepared seed box, remembering to keep the soil constantly moist (but not sodden) until the shoots begin to show. When large enough to handle, plant out the seedlings to about 15 cm (6 in) apart, and keep them moist until well established. Pests and diseases tend to leave the highly aromatic chamomiles well alone.

DRYING

Pick the opened heads carefully with scissors on a clear day, before the sun has drawn the valuable, volatile essences from the blossoms. Spread them out on a wire sieve, or on sheets of paper, in a cool, airy place. When papery-crisp, put the fragrant heads in clean, dry airtight containers for tea or potpourri.

chamomile tea

Using fresh flowers for tea is not as successful as using dried ones. Chamomile mixes well with other herbs, in combinations such as chamomile, fennel and sage, or chamomile and mint.

To make the tea, steep 1 teaspoon of dried chamomile flowers in 1 cup of boiling water for a few minutes and then strain. Sweeten with honey or add lemon to taste.

Try a chamomile cooler by combining a stronger brew of chamomile tea (sweetened with honey to taste) with natural, sparkling mineral water. Add ice-cubes, thin slices of lemon, and float a few whole chamomile flowers on top.

MAKING HERB TEAS

Simply pour boiling water over fresh or dried herbs, allow the brew to infuse, then strain and serve with a slice of lemon, orange or lime for flavour and with honey or sugar to sweeten. You can make the tea directly in the cup, but a teapot is better for very aromatic herbs that have a large amount of volatile oil such as peppermint or rosemary, or for combination teas.

Serving herb tea on ice and adding long leafy stems and sparkling mineral water makes an unbeatable summer cooler.

DRIED HERB LEAVES
Allow about 1 teaspoon dried leaves per cup. Add boiling water and infuse or brew for about 3 minutes.

FRESH HERB LEAVES
Allow 2–3 teaspoons fresh leaves per cup to taste. Add boiling water and brew for 5–6 minutes.

FRESH OR DRIED FLOWERS
Allow about 2 teaspoons per cup. Add boiling water and brew for 5–6 minutes before straining and serving.

SEEDS
To bring out the full flavour of teas made with seeds, crush the seeds slightly before placing them in the teapot to release the volatile oils. Allow $1/2$–1 teaspoon of seeds per cup. Add boiling water and let the brew draw a little longer than usual.

chervil

anthriscus cerefolium

If plants had a gender, then pretty, lacy, delicate, decorative chervil would surely be female! It even blushes, as older leaves take on a reddish glow towards the end of summer. Although it has the same flowering habit as dill, caraway and fennel, its seeds are not used in cooking.

Chervil is one of the four fragrant herbs that make up the delicate *fines herbes* bouquet – the others are chives, tarragon and parsley in equal parts, and all finely chopped. Chervil's soft fresh leaves with their mild aroma, reminiscent of parsley, are an excellent garnish for light-textured foods such as Eggs Benedict, herb sandwiches and salads. They are delicious too, cut finely and folded into scrambled eggs, omelettes, creamed potatoes and cream cheese, sprinkled liberally on salads or used as a filling for sandwiches.

Chervil complements poultry and fish and is excellent over *al dente* vegetables with melted butter and freshly ground pepper and salt. Hold back and only add chervil to the dish or pot at the last minute – it should never be cooked for more than 3–5 minutes, and never at high temperatures, or you will lose the subtlety of its delicate flavour.

Fresh chervil is sometimes available from fruit and vegetable retailers. However, if you like to use it in your cooking, you'll probably have to grow your own and pick it throughout the summer as required. For year-round fresh leaves, freeze finely chopped leaves with a little water in ice-cube trays.

Well aware of the 'don't leave home without it' rule, the Romans took this native of Eastern Europe (it supposedly originated in Siberia) with them as they colonised the Mediterranean world. It has tended to be most popular in French cuisine, but chervil soup is still traditional Holy Thursday fare in many parts of Europe.

GROWING

Chervil rather resembles a miniature parsley plant, although the fern-like leaves are smaller and finer, and it's a brighter green. The white flowers are so minute, it's as though nature knew that the lacy leaves alone would give this herb enough beauty. Chervil is frost-sensitive and needs a sheltered position in colder areas. On the other hand, it also dislikes hot, dry conditions, so you need to protect the plants from the summer sun, too. One solution is to plant chervil near a deciduous tree where it can have the best of both worlds – summer shade and winter sun.

Although sometimes classed as a biennial, it is best to treat chervil as an annual, sowing seeds in spring and in autumn about 30 cm (12 in) apart in a well-prepared garden bed. Never start chervil in a seed box as the seedlings are *much* too delicate to transplant. Cover the seeds with soil and pat down. When the seedlings are about 5 cm (2 in) high, they should be sturdy enough to thin out. Keep them watered at all times and don't forget to feed them occasionally. Or, if that all seems like too much work, just buy nicely established seedlings in little pots at your nursery.

Cochin-style Barbecued Seafood (recipe page 58)

Scrambled Eggs with Fines Herbes (recipe page 41)

Frequent picking encourages new growth and prevents seeding and dying off. Break the stems off carefully, taking the outside leaves first, as with parsley, so that the new centre leaves unfold and grow. Pick and use the foliage as required. If you wish chervil to self-sow, which it will do very readily, do not harvest all the plants when they are in flower; leave about one-third to go to seed.

As chervil only grows to about 30 cm (12 in), it is ideal for pots. Select one that's at least 30 cm (12 in) in diameter, with about 20 cm (8 in) depth for the roots. Fill it with a good quality, porous potting mixture and scatter the seeds over the surface. Press them gently down with a flat piece of board, and lightly sprinkle with water. Keep the pot moist, and when the seedlings are big enough, thin them out.

DRYING

Drying fragile chervil is something of a challenge as the leaves shrivel during dehydration and lose their volatile top notes. Spread the leaves out on a wire rack in a dry, airy, dark place, as light will fade the green colour. Crumble the crisp leaves from the stems, store in airtight, labelled containers and use within three or four months.

scrambled eggs with fines herbes

Serve these creamy scrambled eggs hot from the pan on squares of toast and garnish with fresh chervil sprigs.

4 or 5 x 60 g (2½ oz) eggs
3 tablespoons milk for each egg
salt and pepper
1 teaspoon finely chopped chervil
1 teaspoon finely chopped tarragon
1 teaspoon finely chopped parsley
1 teaspoon finely chopped chives

Fill the bottom half of a double saucepan with enough water to just touch the base of the top half of the saucepan. Bring to a gentle simmer. Break the eggs into a bowl and add the milk, salt and pepper. Whisk to combine, then add the *fines herbes*. Transfer the egg mixture to the top of the double saucepan, and stir frequently until the mixture begins to thicken, about 3 minutes, covering when not stirring. When the eggs thicken, replace the lid and leave to set for about 2 minutes, checking frequently.

Serves 2

chicory

cichorium intybus

If you feel confused about chicory, Belgian endive, witloof (or witlof), don't worry, you are not alone. However, it's essentially one and the same plant in its various herb or vegetable guises. In Belgium, France and Italy this species has produced a whole range of leafy vegetables (including radicchio), all of which have well-established places in those countries' cuisines.

Closely related to the lettuce family (*Lactuca*), chicory is delicious both raw and cooked. The young fresh leaves picked straight from the garden make a crisp, slightly bitter addition to salad greens. If you're prepared to sacrifice your chicory plant, the roots can be steamed as a vegetable, but with such an abundance of root vegetables around, it seems more sensible to hold on to your plant and enjoy the leaves.

Chicory greens are also renowned as excellent fodder for sheep, cows and horses, so the larger leaves that are not suitable for the table can be put to good use keeping your favourite animals in good nick. Otherwise, they can be added to the compost heap.

Today, although we don't necessarily know it, most of us are more familiar with 'chicory' in its commercially grown guise as the vegetable, witloof, which looks rather like an elongated lettuce heart – the whiter the better.

To achieve those tightly folded, compressed, creamy, blanched heads (chicons), young plants are forced in warm, moist dark conditions, in much the same way that fennel bulbs are grown as vegetables. Exposure to light during this process makes the leaves greener and increases their bitterness. Chefs pick the fattest, firmest and creamiest specimens.

If you find the flavour of raw witloof leaves on the bitter side, try pouring boiling water over them in a colander before using. Crisped in icy water, these compact, shapely leaves make nifty scoops for dips and fresh salsas.

Witloof is ideal for baking or braising. Try cooking whole (or halved) heads, wrapping each in a piece of ham, arranging them in a lightly buttered gratin dish in a single layer, topping the lot with a creamy bechamel sauce and baking for about 15 minutes until just bubbling and lightly golden on top.

GROWING

Although your greengrocer will call it witloof, you'll find at the garden shop or plant nursery that this herb is more likely to be identified as chicory.

Left alone, chicory is one of the taller herbs with broad, long lower leaves rather like spinach leaves. The higher leaves are smaller and sparser, growing on branching stems, and are not usually eaten.

Chicory is not a plant for a pot, growing to about 1.8 metres (6 feet) in the right conditions. Above the fairly prosaic lower leaves, a flurry of thinner stems form a crown where daisy-like flowers grow in clusters, two or three along the stems, bursting open in the morning sun. The starry blooms have finely serrated, pale blue petals radiating from dark blue stamens. They are very popular with bees – but the bees have to be up early, as the flowers usually close by noon, unless the day is very dull.

This frost-hardy herb likes a sunny position with well-drained soil. Plant the seeds or seedlings in the garden in spring about 30 cm (12 in) apart. Keep watered until the shoots appear, and watch out for those gourmet snails, slugs and caterpillars. Rust fungus and mildew can be a problem too.

DRYING

Pick chicory leaves off the stems and spread them out on a wire rack or insect screen in a cool, airy place away from the light. Crumble the crisp leaves and store in airtight, labelled containers.

Drying, roasting and grinding chicory roots is a commercial procedure that is usually carried out by manufacturers with the appropriate kiln-drying equipment.

a coffee substitute too ...

The roasted root of the chicory plant has been used as a caffeine-free coffee substitute or additive since about 1800, and it had a bit of a resurgence in the Depression and war years of the 1930s and 1940s, when it was mixed with coffee to make a coffee essence.

TURNING CHICORY INTO WITLOOF

If you want to try your hand at growing your own witloof ('blanched' chicory), here's how. Dig out the roots in autumn, about six months after planting.

Cut off the foliage and stand the roots upright, close together, in a deep box or pot, with a covering of light, sandy soil to about 15 cm (6 in) above the top of the roots.

Keep the plants in a moist, dark place such as a warm shed, laundry or garage. As they grow, the new young leaves will become elongated and blanched. If it's not dark enough, the foliage turns green and bitter.

As soon as the white leaves show above the soil the plants are ready for lifting. Cut the root away, leaving just enough at the base to hold the leaves together. Use as soon as possible as witloof deteriorates quickly.

witloof stuffed with pork and prawns

125 g (4½ oz) peeled green prawns
125 g (4½ oz) minced pork
1 spring onion (scallion), finely chopped
½ teaspoon chilli powder
1 clove garlic, crushed
salt and pepper to taste
½ teaspoon ground allspice
1 tablespoon vegetable oil
2 heads of young, crisp witloof, leaves separated

De-vein the prawns and chop them very finely. Place all the ingredients, except the witloof, in a large mixing bowl and combine thoroughly. Heat the oil in a large frying-pan or wok and stir-fry the mixture until the pork and prawns are cooked. Remove from the heat and allow to cool to room temperature.

Soak the leaves in a bowl of icy water until crisp. Drain well and carefully pat each one dry. Spoon the just cool meat mixture into the witloof boats and serve as finger-food.

Serves 3–4 as an entrée

wilted witloof with sesame oil and pine nuts

2 tablespoons pine nuts
2 heads of witloof, or about 20 chicory leaves
    from the garden
1 tablespoon sesame oil
salt to taste

Place the pine nuts in a hot, dry frying pan, and toast until they turn golden brown. Shake the pan constantly so the pine nuts colour evenly. Transfer the pine nuts to a dish and set aside.

Separate the heads of chicory into individual leaves. Heat the sesame oil in a frying pan, add the leaves and cook over a medium heat until they are just wilted. Add the pine nuts to the pan, season with a little salt and toss to combine with the chicory leaves. Serve immediately.

Serves 2

chives

ONION CHIVES *allium schoenoprasum*

GARLIC CHIVES *a. tuberosum*

Chives go with eggs the way salt goes with pepper – it's hard to imagine one without the other. 'Garnish with snipped chives' has long been a culinary catch cry, and tying tiny bundles of French beans with a chive 'spear' is a clear indication that you have gone to a lot of trouble. (Do it for your in-laws.)

Chives are the smallest members of the onion family but it's the leaf, not the bulb, that packs the punch. There are two types of chive, onion and garlic, and they are easy to tell apart. Onion chives are the tubular ones that resemble tufts of fine grass; garlic (or Chinese) chives have flat, rather blade-like leaves.

Because chives don't contain as much sulphur as onion, their subtle flavour is just right in many dishes where onion would overpower. Finely chopped chives go into egg dishes, cream cheese, fish and poultry dishes, savoury sauces, mayonnaise and just about every kind of salad. Try them in a creamy mushroom sauce for serving with penne or your favourite pasta.

One important tip when using chives is not to wash them until you are about to use them as moisture promotes decay. And add chives during the last 5 or so minutes of cooking as their flavour is destroyed with long heating.

Garlic chives are widely used throughout Asia in soups, noodle dishes and with seafood and pork. 'Yellow chives' have a much milder, delicate onion flavour and are obtained by growing garlic chives without sunlight.

Fresh chives are sold in bunches about 2.5 cm (1 in) in diameter, often wrongly labelled – onion chives labelled as garlic and vice versa. Don't buy them if they look wilted.

If you are growing your own chives, pick off the leaves at the base with your fingers, as cutting with scissors causes them to die back slightly and leaves an unattractive brown edge. Chives will keep for about a week stored in a plastic bag in the refrigerator. Fresh chives, both onion- and garlic-flavoured, may be chopped finely, mixed with a little water, and frozen in ice-cube trays to be thawed when needed.

GROWING

Onion chives grow to about 30 cm (12 in) and have tubular hollow leaves like drinking straws. Their charming lavender pompom flowers are actually thick knots of cylindrical petals forming round heads like clover blossoms. The flowers are edible as well, however once chives have flowered, their flavour changes. As with most herbs, the stem that will bear the flower is visibly different (thicker as a rule), so prevent flowers forming by removing the stalk as soon as it appears.

Garlic chives grow to about 60 cm (24 in) and their flowers form white star-like clusters at the top of long, round strong and tough stems.

There are some important guidelines for successful chive growing. First of all, never let the clump grow too large, as the centre will die out from lack of nourishment. If the base of your clump is as wide as the open end of a teacup, it's time to dig it up and divide into four or five smaller clumps.

Chives can also die of exhaustion – they simply disappear if allowed to flower too much. So pick off flower buds as they appear (literally nipping them in the bud) and you will be rewarded with healthy plants as long as you water them well and dig a little decayed manure into the soil occasionally. For a continuous supply, pick chives about 5 cm (2 in) above the ground rather than pulling them out by the roots.

You can buy chives as established plants, as seeds, or divide the roots from an older clump. They will grow year round in a sunny position, but not very vigorously in winter. Sow seeds in a seed box in spring in fairly rich well-drained soil. When the seedlings have passed the point where they look like delicate grass, plant them out in the garden, or in 15 cm (6 in) diameter pots. They will be happy on a sunny exterior windowsill. Because chives form a small bulb, allow about 12 bulbs to a clump when planting, keeping the clumps 30 cm (12 in) apart. In winter the tops of chives tend to wither; then they shoot again in spring making this the best time to divide the clumps – about 5 cm (2 in) in diameter.

Aphids find chives totally irresistible, which is why chives are sometimes planted with roses, to act as a decoy for these pests. If you're averse to using pesticides, adjust your hose nozzle to a firm jet and blast the aphids off the chives. Mind you, it won't stop them coming back!

DRIED CHIVES

Don't even to begin to give yourself the heartache of trying to dry your own chives. Drying chives in the normal way is not satisfactory as they lose their colour and flavour. The chives that one buys in bottles from the supermarket are probably onion chives and will have been freeze dried. The cell structure and colour are so delicate that once you have bought freeze-dried chives, you have to keep them in the dark (they are inordinately light sensitive) or they will fade very quickly.

summer carrot and chive salad

This summery salad has become something of a family staple. We discovered it in Jane Grigson's wonderful book, *Good Things,* first published in 1971, and we have adapted it over the years to suit our enthusiasm for chives and preference for a sharper dressing. Jane Grigson is absolutely right when she says it is the easiest dish in the world to prepare. And everyone always comes back for seconds.

6 medium-sized carrots (choose bright orange ones), peeled and grated
1 bunch chives, snipped (use more if you like)
2–3 tablespoons extra virgin olive oil
juice of 1 lemon
pinch sea salt
sugar to taste

Combine all the ingredients adding the salt and sugar to taste. Chill for about an hour then gently turn the mass of carrots over with a fork. If the salad seems to be swimming in liquid, drain it before serving.

Serves 4–6 as an accompaniment

fines herbes

The classic blend of delicately flavoured herbs known as *fines herbes* consists of onion chives, chervil, parsley and tarragon. These herbs are finely chopped and mixed together in equal quantities making a delightfully mild, savoury blend to flavour omelettes, cooked chicken and fish, salads, steamed vegetables, soups, and mornay dishes.

coriander

coriandrum sativum

Coriander (known as cilantro in the Americas), with its delicate green foliage, has an air of innocence. But don't be misled, this herb is a heartbreaker. We have seen people in tears as they relate the sad tale of how their healthy plant suddenly turned up its toes and died for no apparent reason. The awful truth is that this annual is the shortest-lived of all, with a hasty life cycle of grow-flower-seed-die within a short couple of months. Do you really think market gardeners would pull the plant out, roots and all, if there were a chance of a second harvest? (Does that taproot remind you of a carrot? Yes, it's a member of the same family.)

Many herbs, such as anise, caraway, dill and fennel, have, in varying degrees, the same warm, spicy, anise pungency. However, the unique flavour of fresh coriander leaves also carries hints of lemon peel and sage. From its home base in Southern Europe, the aromatic leaves and spicy mature seeds of this international traveller have made themselves indispensable.

If you are looking for flavour and value for money you can't go past coriander because you can eat the whole herb.

The leaves have the strongest flavour, though it is quickly diffused with cooking. They are best added at the last minute or they can become bitter. Consequently coriander is frequently used to garnish Asian and Indian stir-fries and curries, hence the nickname 'Chinese parsley', coined by those of European heritage who use the ubiquitous parsley sprig to garnish everything from eggs to sandwiches to goulash.

The stems don't have as much flavour as the leaves, but finely chopped are a crispy addition to stir-fries and clear Asian soups, perhaps combined with garlic and lemongrass. The same applies to the grated roots.

Coriander is a key ingredient in curries, tagines, ceviche, gumbos, and in past times was even added to the centre of rainbow balls, to give a unique piquancy.

In Mexican food, coriander is always used fresh. The cilantro/coriander question has confused countless Australian cooks following American recipes, but the answer is easy – in American recipes, cilantro refers to the leaves, and coriander to the seed or powder; pretty much everywhere else, it's all called coriander.

Coriander leaves are widely used in Cajun cooking, where seasoning is all. Traditional Louisiana gumbos may contain any combination of okra, seafood, meat or vegetables, with seasonings of chopped fresh herbs including cilantro, garlic, parsley, bay leaves, basil, thyme or fennel – whichever the cook fancies.

South America's seafood ceviche with capsicum (bell peppers), Spanish onion, lemons and limes wouldn't be the same without fresh coriander. To make a good ceviche, the seafood and all the other ingredients must be absolutely fresh including citrus juice, peppers, onions, and a choice of vegetables. Finely chopped coriander is used in nearly all the recipes, sometimes with parsley as well.

If you are growing your own coriander, pick leaves fresh at any time. As with other delicate herbs, fresh leaves provide the best flavour and frequent picking will encourage growth and prevent the plant from going to seed. To freeze, wrap freshly washed sprays in foil, folding the edges in securely. They will keep for several weeks in the freezer. The ice-cube tray method isn't appropriate for coriander.

When you buy fresh coriander, make sure that you buy it in bunches with the root system intact as this will keep it fresh longer. To store, stand the bunch in a glass of water in the refrigerator. Pull a plastic bag down over the leaves and fold under the base of the glass to make its own little igloo of humidity so that the leaves don't dry out. If you discard the leaves as they turn yellow the coriander should last for a week or two.

GROWING

Coriander likes sun and shelter as the young plants need protection from prevailing winds to prevent them from falling over. If you don't have an obviously sheltered spot, try planting it in the garden among the other plants. Work the soil until it is fine and crumbly, adding a little lime if the ground is acid. Plant coriander seedlings (or sow the seeds) in spring or summer (and again in autumn in temperate zones) about 30 cm (12 in) apart directly in the garden – it has a taproot that doesn't like being transplanted. Cover the seeds and pack the soil down well, then keep moist until the seedlings appear. Water regularly in hot, dry weather, preferably in the late afternoon or evening so as not to scorch the plants. As they grow, they may need staking.

In high summer conditions, coriander has a tendency to bolt, going to seed almost as soon as it has reached maturity. To prevent this, nip off the thick flower-bearing stems as soon as you see them, and this way you can delay the inevitable blooms for a week or two. The alternative is to allow the flowers and seeds to develop and drop, so that new plants will self-sow, giving you a continuing supply of leaves.

The mauve-tinted white blossoms appear in summer in frothy profusion, followed by fruit, which, when green and unripened, have an even stronger scent than the foliage. When the small, oval coriander seeds have hardened and ripened to a pale fawn colour, they are one of the most deliciously fragrant of all spices used in cooking.

DRYING

Cut leafy stalks for drying, pick off the individual leaves and spread them out in a shady place on wire mesh to encourage quick drying. Do not hang them in bunches, as the soft foliage will then dry too slowly and may possibly spoil. Oven or microwave drying is not satisfactory, as the leaves bruise easily and are liable to scorch. When crisp, crumble the leaves from the stalks and store in airtight containers.

To test the quality of dry coriander leaves, place a few on your tongue and wait for the flavour to emerge. Dried leaves can be used in stir-fries or added in the last couple of minutes of cooking time, but they are not suitable for garnishing.

To harvest the seeds, cut off all the heads when they are about to drop, and dry them, like ripe anise, on sheets of paper in a shady place, exposing them to the sun when possible. They are ready to store when the fruit falls away from the shrivelled flower heads if given a light shake. Sieve out any pieces of stalk, and pack the seeds into airtight containers.

kate's fantastic fresh spring rolls

Like Ian, our daughter Kate has grown up surrounded by the flavour and aroma of herbs. She is now making her mark in the family business with her fresh and exciting recipes. These spring rolls can be prepared ahead of time and arranged on a platter ready to serve. Simply cover and refrigerate until you need them. Serve with sweet chilli or peanut sauce.

1 x 100 g (3½ oz) portion of vermicelli rice noodles

1 bunch coriander (cilantro)

½ bunch mint

¼ iceberg lettuce, chopped

½ red capsicum (bell pepper), finely diced

1 Lebanese cucumber, peeled and finely diced

1 tablespoon sweet chilli sauce

1 packet rice paper squares or rounds

Soak the rice noodles in warm water until soft, then drain well. Pick the coriander and mint leaves from the stems and chop them roughly. Place all the ingredients (except the rice paper squares) in a large mixing bowl and combine thoroughly.

Soak the rice papers, one at a time, in a bowl of warm water. After 15–20 seconds they will be pliable. Carefully spread the rice papers on a damp chopping board. Place a spoonful of mixture in the lower part of the paper. Carefully fold the edges in then fold the bottom up and roll them tightly.

Makes about 20 spring rolls

coriander dipping sauce

A lovely tangy dipping sauce to serve with fresh peeled king prawns.

Makes about 1 cup

1 bunch coriander (cilantro), leaves picked

1 bunch mint, leaves picked

1 bunch spring onions (scallions), roughly chopped

2 cm (¾ in) piece of fresh ginger, peeled

juice of 1 lime

250 g (9 oz) plain yoghurt

salt and pepper to taste

Blend the coriander, mint, spring onions and ginger in a food processor to make a smooth paste. Add the lime juice and yoghurt to the paste, and stir to combine. Season with salt and pepper to taste.

powder to paste

To make a quick curry paste, lightly fry some finely chopped onion and garlic in oil, add the curry powder of your choice and enough water to make a paste. For a richer and redder brew, add tomato paste to taste. And for extra flavour add chopped fresh coriander and use a little tamarind water (made by soaking a piece of tamarind pulp in water and straining). Keep refrigerated and use within 5 days.

cress

WATERCRESS *nasturtium officinale*

CURLED CRESS AND FRENCH CRESS *lepidium sativatum*

AMERICAN UPLAND CRESS *barbarea vulgaris*

People commonly think that the only type of cress is the watercress that grows wild in fresh flowing streams or babbling brooks. However, there are several cress varieties, all rich in iron and all from the *Cruciferae* family, famous for having no poisonous plants among its two thousand-odd species.

Watercress can grow in soil too, as long as it is planted in shade and kept damp. In fact it is easy to grow and its biting taste spikes summer salads, makes refreshing chilled soups and substitutes for spinach in quiches, frittatas, dips and eggs Florentine. You can get a less pungent result by combining cress with spinach in a ratio of about 1 to 4.

Watercress is a hardy perennial with small, round, dark green leaves and tiny white flowers and its taste is rather peppery, like nasturtium. In fact the true nasturtium with its creeping habit and show of flowers is sometimes called Indian cress.

Land cress has a similar flavour, and the best-known species are the curled, French and American upland cress.

Curled cress looks rather like curled parsley, but its leaves are fleshier and the flavour is hot and sharp. You can sprout this cress indoors on trays without soil, cutting before it matures into a fully-grown plant and serving with its lifelong chum, mustard.

French cress resembles young lettuce with undivided pale-green leaves with a frilled edge. It may not look at all like the other cresses, but its leaves have the same pepper-hot bite.

American upland cress has long leaves like a dandelion forming a full rosette of dark-green jagged leaves up to 15 cm (6 in) long, with a typically hot flavour.

Fresh cress leaves are best for flavour and appearance. You can chop the leaves finely, mix them with a little water and freeze them in ice-cube trays for adding to soups and stews at the end of cooking time. Sprigs of cress may be wrapped in foil, sealed, and kept in the deep freeze for some weeks.

GROWING

The old suggestion that watercress needs flowing water to survive is wrong. It seems to be just as happy in the garden or in a container. But although it may not need that babbling brook, it does need fresh water (not stagnant) as well as soil for growing. So, if you don't happen to have natural spring water nearby, a shallow trough where you can change the water will do just fine. In fact, plant it in a damp, shady place, or stand a pot in a tray of water, and watch it thrive!

The first step is to sow the seeds in spring or autumn in a prepared seed box. When the seedlings are big enough to handle, transfer them to the shallow trough, half filled with loamy soil. Place the trough under a tap in semi-shade, and as the seedlings grow, gradually fill the trough with water, carefully draining it about once a week and refilling it with fresh water. The more cress is cut, the more it will branch. In summer, frequent cutting will prevent flowering and assure plenty of leafiness for harvesting.

Grow all land cresses the same way, as annuals. Sow the seeds in a semi-shady part of the garden virtually year-round, unless you are in an area that gets frosts, about 2 cm (¾ in) apart straight into what will be their permanent home. Apart from watering in dry weather, there is no need for any special attention. Just dig in a little fertiliser from time to time. Germination is rewardingly speedy (about a week), which is why cress is very popular with beginning gardeners. Plants should be ready for harvesting in about four weeks although they can take longer in cooler climes – like many plants, cress does not thrive in frosty conditions. Once the plants have reached 10–15 cm (4–6 in) tall, cut them to just above ground level with a pair of scissors.

DRYING

Cress is a difficult herb to dry, and really, why bother when it's so readily available fresh?

For herb teas, dry watercress leaves on an airy rack, and when crisp, crumble into airtight containers.

watercress sandwiches

If you cut the bread corner-to-corner into triangles the cheese and cress mixture makes enough for 40 small sandwiches. Simply arrange on a platter and serve. Use a good grainy bread sliced as thinly as possible at your bread shop and allow one tightly packed cup of fresh watercress leaves per loaf (about 20 slices).

1 tightly packed cup of fresh watercress
   leaves, finely chopped
1 cup cheese spread (or cottage cheese,
   ricotta or cream cheese)
20 slices of a good grainy bread, sliced as thinly as possible

Mix the leaves with your preferred soft cheese. Spread the slices generously with the mixture, make into sandwiches and remove the crusts if you prefer.

SPROUTING

Sprouts are seeds that have been brought to life with water and allowed to develop a soft green shoot. They are very easy to grow and ready to eat within a week. And you can eat them roots and all – they are a complete, living food.

There are a couple of standard methods for sprouting and they work for cress seeds, lentils, mung beans, Chinese beans, alfalfa and mustard seeds.

One method is to take an empty jar about the size of a honey jar and a piece of thin material or a strip cut from tights or stockings. Put 2 teaspoons of cress seeds (or whatever you want to sprout) in the jar, stretch the gauzy fabric over the top and hold it in place with a rubber band. Now add a little water and let the seeds soak for a minute or so before straining. Shake the jar to make sure all the excess water is out, and lie it on its side away from direct sunshine. Water every morning and evening following the same procedure and watch your cress seeds turn into tender shoots. Tuck in when you see the first tender leaves.

Alternatively, place a layer of cotton wool or paper towel on a plate and sprinkle the seeds on top. Water and watch your seeds grow and harvest them as they sprout.

curry tree

murraya koenigii

Chicken Salad with Lemon Balm and Thai Spices (recipe page 16)

Warm Minted Lamb and Tomato Salad (recipe page 109)

Although they don't exactly taste of curry, the neat, spicy leaves of the curry tree bring a tantalising, fresh aroma and flavour to curries. Rather than echoing the flavour of curry, they complement it, gaining their name by this happy association.

The leaves are more pungent fresh than dried and it is almost impossible to use too many in a curry or South-East Asian dish. For maximum flavour when curry making, gently cook the leaves in a little oil first. Whole leaves are also perfect for pickle-making or adding to seafood marinades. Crushed they can be added to curry pastes and powders. To create a truly professional presentation of an Indian dish, top it with a little cluster of crispy, deep-fried curry leaves.

Fresh leaves will keep in a plastic bag in the refrigerator for a week. Good quality dried leaves are hard to find, but it's not impossible to dry your own with a little care.

The curry tree is absolutely unrelated to the curry plant (*Helichrysum angustifolium*) with its silvery-grey foliage. Although there are those who claim its leaves have a curry aroma and flavour, we don't consider this to be a culinary herb at all (which is why we haven't written about it in this book). Just for the record, it's an oregano-sized plant suitable for garden edges.

GROWING

The evergreen curry tree is a native of India and Sri Lanka and belongs to the citrus family. Its shiny, frond-like leaves grow to 3–7 cm (1½–3 in) long and 1–2 cm (½–¾ in) wide. Although it is a tropical plant, the curry tree does well in a sunny spot in sub-tropical and temperate zones when well protected from frost and wind.

Curry trees thrive in well-drained soil that's rich in organic matter in a raised bed or large tub, but bear in mind that it grows to about 4 metres (13 feet). Prune lightly in the autumn so that the buds for new spring growth have time to establish.

In summer, clusters of tiny white flowers are followed by small, blue-black, edible fruits, which will self-sow around the base of your tree if you're lucky. Suckers or runners, spreading from the parent root base, provide a much more satisfactory method of propagation than planting cuttings or seeds. And it is much quicker.

In the tropics the leaves are there for the picking year-round, however in places where winters are colder, your tree might lose its leaves or look rather sick, completely contradicting the evergreen label it adopts in the tropics.

Some trees develop miserable-looking dark spots on the leaves, some turn completely yellow, some drop every single leaf. Don't despair, as beautiful new growth will gladden your heart when the days warm up.

DRYING

If you take care when drying the leaves, you will find that they retain more of their colour and flavour. Strip healthy green leaves from the main stem (don't take the youngest ones), and spread them out in a single layer on paper or wire gauze in a dark, airy, warm, dry place – with zero humidity if possible. When the leaves are crisp and dry, store in labelled airtight containers.

cochin-style barbecued seafood

For a moister, more succulent result, wrap the prawns and bug tails in foil before barbecuing.

2 tablespoons grated onion
6–8 curry leaves, crumbled
1 teaspoon garam masala
1/8 teaspoon medium chilli powder
1/2 teaspoon salt
8 king prawns
2 Balmain bug tails (jumbo shrimp), halved

Purée the onion and curry leaves to make a paste (add a little water if it's too dry to purée), then add garam masala, chilli powder and salt. Combine with the peeled prawns and bug tails in a bowl and mix until the seafood is well coated. Let stand for 30 minutes then cook on the barbecue griddle.

Serves 2

herbie's kerala chicken stir-fry

This spicy mix is also delicious with fish fillets such as ling or fresh green prawns. In India they would use coconut oil, but we suggest you opt for a polyunsaturated vegetable oil.

1 onion, diced
1 tablespoon vegetable oil
1 tablespoon garam masala
1/2 teaspoon medium chilli powder, more if you prefer
20 fresh curry leaves
1/2 teaspoon salt
4 fillets skinless chicken, sliced

Blend the onion, oil, garam masala, chilli powder, curry leaves and salt to make a paste. Coat the chicken slices with the mixture, cover and set aside in the refrigerator for about 30 minutes. Stir-fry until cooked and serve with steamed rice.

Serves 6

dill

anethum graveolens

Smoked salmon just wouldn't be the same without those ever-so-feathery refreshing dill tips, which not only garnish but add a flavour zing as well. This frond-like herb with its subtle anise aroma belongs to the far-flung *Apiaceae* family that also includes kissing cousins anise, caraway, coriander, cumin and parsley.

Refreshing is the word that perfectly describes dill; it's a summer thing. Finely chopped dill leaves bring their palate-pleasing liveliness to cottage or cream cheese, omelettes, white sauce, salads and dressings, cucumber, seafood, chicken, rice, egg dishes, soups, steamed vegetables and infused herb vinegars.

When you buy dill, it's pretty hard to find a bunch that is not wilting, because it's a delicate creature and doesn't like lying around in a shop. Choose the best you can find, and when you get it home, immerse the entire bunch in a bowl of water and keep it in the fridge. The leaves will crisp up in the cold water, but try to use it as soon as possible after purchasing it.

For freezing, chop the fresh leaves finely, mix with a little water, and put into ice-cube trays in the freezer. Sprays of fresh dill may be wrapped in foil, sealed, and kept in the deep freeze for some weeks.

The seeds have a more robust aroma than the tips and are used to flavour cabbage, coleslaw, sauerkraut, cucumbers, onions, chutneys and pickles, breads, sauces and root vegetables, especially in Russia, Germany and Scandinavia. Anyone over a certain age will associate dill seeds with dill water, an infusion of dill seeds, which used to be given to babies for colic. One has to wonder what babies thought of that anise flavour – no wonder they cried!

GROWING

Dill looks rather like fennel but has darker leaves and is smaller, growing to about 90 cm (36 in) tall and 40 cm (16 in) wide in a sunny spot. The slender central stems are easily flattened by wind, so grow the plants in a sheltered position in light, well-drained soil.

In temperate areas, you can do two plantings a year – one in spring, and another in autumn. As the soft, delicate seedlings do not transplant easily, sow the seeds (or plant seedlings) directly into the garden about 25 cm (10 in) apart. Gently cover, firm down the soil and water well. If the soil is sour, lime it well first. An occasional feed of a good organic fertiliser will pay leafy dividends – but if you're keen on chook manure, it must be well composted and dry. To keep those feathery tips coming throughout the summer, pick leaves from the centre to delay flowering.

Dill will be happy either in the garden or in a pot, but watch out for aphids as they tend to zoom in on this little herb, and can even kill it if they are in heavy numbers. Ladybirds are a natural predator of aphids, so only spray as a final resort or you'll chase away the cure as well as the pest.

In the summer, dill bears pale yellow umbelliferous flower heads, like those of anise and fennel, made up of about 20 tiny florets that form oval, flat seeds in abundance in late summer and autumn. Dill seeds – which are actually the minute fruit divided in two – are about 4 mm (¼ in) long. They ripen in autumn and can be collected as soon as the first few fall.

DRYING

To make the most of these aromatic, anise-tasting leaves, cut the feathery fresh green tips just as the flower buds start to form. Spread them out on a piece of absorbent paper such as kitchen paper towel and place in a warm, well-aired, dark place for a few days to dry. They will feel crisp when they are dry. To retain the lovely green colour, store them in a cupboard in an airtight container rather than an open spice rack.

You can also dry dill successfully in a microwave oven. Place the tips on a piece of kitchen paper towel in the oven with half a cup of water in a microwave-safe cup and cook on high for a couple of minutes then check. Continue to cook in 30-second bursts until the leaves feel crisp and dry.

To collect and dry the seeds, snip off the heads when the flowers have finished and spread them out on a tray in the sun for a few days. When they are completely dry, the seeds shake out easily from the heads. You might like to winnow the seeds or sieve them to remove any little pieces of dry flower or stem, then store your harvest in airtight containers. If you wish to re-sow dill seed, it should be done within three years for good germinating results.

smoked salmon with capers and dill

'Refreshing' perfectly describes the flavour of dill, as well as these tasty toasts with smoked salmon or trout slices and capers.

3 slices wholemeal bread, crusts removed
2 tablespoons mayonnaise mixed with an extra teaspoon
    chopped dill
200 g (7 oz) smoked salmon slices or smoked trout, flaked
24 capers
fresh dill tips

Roll the bread slices gently with a rolling pin to flatten until they are about half their original thickness. Toast the slices until golden, and cut each into quarters – in squares or triangles. Top each piece with a dollop of mayonnaise, a generous serving of salmon, a couple of drained capers, and a sprinkle of dill tips. Serve immediately.

Makes 12

elder

sambucus nigra

This fascinating tree was long regarded as the medicine chest of country people, and it was not only the berries and flowers that they put to use. The close-grained white wood of old trees was cut and polished and made into butchers' skewers, shoemakers' pegs, needles for weaving nets, combs, mathematical instruments, and some musical instruments. The stems, with pith removed, made whistles and popguns for country boys.

The European (black or common) elder is the one to grow in a herb garden, although you would probably need to have two or three trees to provide sufficient flowers and berries to make wine. From late summer, filmy heads of creamy-white flowers put bees in nectar-heaven. Birds have their turn for feasting in autumn, when drooping bunches of rich garnet-coloured berries cover the tree in prolific splendour.

The uses of the flowers and berries are legion. However, unlike the birds and the bees, we humans generally prefer our elderflowers and berries processed first! The minute petals make infusions for cordials and teas and the fresh flowers are used for wine.

Elderberries have been used for centuries to make wine, but today they are more often used to colour conventional wines, particularly some ports produced in Portugal. Tasting rather like blackcurrants, elderberries add a distinctive sharpness to jams, jellies, fruit tarts and apple sauce. They are also used on their own to make jam, jelly, chutney and ketchup.

GROWING

Elder is a deciduous tree with finely serrated leaves advancing in pairs along supple, pale green stems that cling to bronze, woody branches. It grows to around 4–6 metres (13–20 feet) tall, with a dense spreading habit that can quickly become an impenetrable thicket in the right growing conditions.

Elder trees are hardy and will grow almost anywhere, but they do best in rich, moist soil. If for some reason you want a grove of trees, leave at least 3–4 metres (10–13 feet) between each one. However be warned, because of their suckering habit, you'll have a solid jungle rather than a grove if you're not prepared to be vigilant and act. They are fond of moisture and partial to a sunny position with semi-shade, though they will soldier on regardless if you forget to water them for a while. They should be cut back hard in winter (remember that spreading habit).

Back in the Somerset Cottage days, John reported the greatest success in propagating by taking 15 cm (6 in) hardwood cuttings in late winter before the spring shoots appeared, and putting them in a container of river sand. Tip cuttings can also be struck in river sand in late spring when the new growth has firmed. When roots appear the cuttings can be planted out, or put into containers with potting mixture. It is also possible to strike cuttings of sprouting wood in early spring in the open ground. Suckers, with some root from the main plant attached, can be dug and transplanted throughout the year, unless winters are harsh, when you may lose them.

If you should decide that you no longer want your elder tree, or that you'd rather it was somewhere else in your garden, it's too bad. We tried in vain to kill an unwanted elder tree for years, first chopping it out (we thought), then burning out the stump (we thought) and finally in desperation, hitting it with Round-Up. It outlasted our days at Grose Vale. And while we have moved on, as far as we know, 15-plus years later, it's still there, growing strong.

DRYING

Gather the blooms when all the tiny buds on each pearly cluster are open, and do this by midday before the sun draws out too much of the flower's etheric substance.

Put the heads somewhere shady to dry – a sheet of paper in a warm dry place – and when they shrivel, and look like fine, yellowed crochet, remove them to make room for more fresh flowers. Store the dried ones whole in airtight boxes or jars, or rub them from their frail stalks first. Leave some flowers on the trees for using fresh and to ensure that there will be some fruit later.

When the shiny green berries form, watch them ripen and pick them as they begin to turn reddish purple. If it is not convenient to use the berries at once, allow them to dry, and store in airtight containers. They keep their flavour well and are used like dried currants.

elderflower fritters

8 elderflower heads

1 tablespoon orange-flower water

1 teaspoon ground cinnamon

½ cup light-flavoured unsaturated oil, or more if necessary

1 or 2 tablespoons caster (superfine) sugar

Batter

3 tablespoons plain (all-purpose) flour

1 tablespoon cornflour (cornstarch)

½ tablespoon caster (superfine) sugar

1 egg, separated

around 1 cup milk

Place the flower heads in a bowl and sprinkle with orange-flower water and cinnamon.

To make the batter, sift the flours into a large bowl and stir in the sugar. Mix the egg yolk with ½ cup of the milk and stir into the dry ingredients. Add more milk, bit by bit, until the batter is smooth and of a thick pouring consistency. Whisk the egg white to soft peaks in a clean bowl (to make the batter as light and airy as the flowers themselves) and fold into the batter.

To make the fritters, heat the oil in a small deep saucepan. Dip the elderflowers into the batter, one at a time, and deep-fry them in the hot oil. As soon as the fritters colour, remove them from the oil. Drain on kitchen towel for a couple of minutes, then arrange on a platter, sprinkle with caster sugar and serve while hot with clotted cream.

Makes 8

fennel

foeniculum vulgare

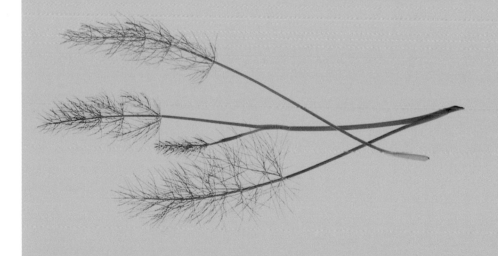

All things to all people – that's fennel (also known as Florence fennel, common fennel or sweet fennel). You want a vegetable, a herb, a spice, a garnish? Then fennel's the one for you. The feathery, dark green leaves have an anise aroma similar to that of dill, and the prolific umbels of summery yellow flowers make way for juicy plump seeds that are delicious eaten straight from the garden. Sometimes these seeds are referred to as the fruit of the fennel, which in a way is technically correct; however, if you plant it and it grows, it's a seed.

The fragrant leaves have a delicate flavour and are best fresh. They are used very much the same way as their little cousin dill – in salads, sauces, with all kinds of seafood and to garnish terrines, soups and aspic. Pick a lavish bunch of fresh fennel to make an aromatic bed for baking a whole fish.

Like so many other fresh herbs, chopped fresh fennel can be made into ice-blocks for later use, and sprigs of fresh fennel can be wrapped in foil, sealed, and kept in the freezer for up to a month.

The bulb is a serious contender for the 'versatile vegetable' prize. It is delicious whatever you do with it: sliced fresh for crisp-textured salads, added to stews, simply steamed, served with a light sauce or quartered and baked Italian-style with a little nutmeg, butter and garlic and topped with sizzling freshly grated parmesan cheese.

The seeds, whole or ground, can be added to soup, breads, spicy sausages, pasta, tomato dishes, sauerkraut and salads. Watch out for Italian specialties such as *taralini* (savoury biscuits) showing anise as an ingredient – in fact it's fennel. It's a sad fact that poor old fennel doesn't get the recognition it deserves – you'll often see fennel bulbs beautifully displayed in fruit and vegetable shops and wrongly labelled 'aniseed'. Try to convince anyone to call it otherwise, and you're up against generations of habit and you'll never win.

In Indian and Asian cooking the seeds are often lightly roasted before being added to curries and satay sauces, or sugar-coated and served as a sweet, liquorice-flavoured digestive. You can find these treats at Indian provision stores or at a good spice shop.

GROWING

Because fennel is an annual, it will die away in winter and needs to be replanted again each year. If you have plenty of space, plant seedlings (or seeds) in late spring or early summer about 30 cm (12 in) apart straight into a sunny part of the garden. A rich, well-drained soil will give the best results and you may need to fertilise occasionally. Fennel grows to about 90 cm (36 in) , so it is perfectly suitable for potting – just make sure your pot is at least 30 cm (12 in) deep so that there's room for the bulb. Remember to give your plant plenty of water to encourage lots of bright green foliage.

The fennel bulbs sold as vegetables have been specially treated so that they grow beyond their natural size. When the bulb is as big as a golf ball, heap some soil up around it, continually adding more as it grows, to keep the bulb covered. Remove the flower heads as they appear. When the bulbs are large enough to use, cut them away from the roots, tie them together by the foliage and hang in a dry place. Use within 10 days after cutting, otherwise you will lose the fresh, crisp texture. For using in salads, cover the bulb in a bowl of water in the fridge for a while to get maximum crispness.

DRYING

Don't even bother trying to dry the fragile, wispy leaves. There are too sappy and by the time they have dried, most of the flavour will be lost.

Drying the seeds is quite easy. Allow them to develop and ripen in autumn, then clip off the heads and tie them together by the stems. Hang the bunch in an airy, shady place with clean paper or cloth spread underneath to catch any seeds that fall. After a few days, hold the bunch by the stems and shake out all the seeds. Store them in an airtight container, and delight in their freshness as you use them. Try grinding a few teaspoons of them and sprinkling over tuna fillets, then brush the fish with olive oil and grill – yum!

risotto with garlic and fennel

8–10 strands saffron
2½ cups chicken stock, kept simmering
freshly ground black pepper
1–2 tablespoons olive oil
1 small onion, finely chopped
4–5 cloves garlic, finely chopped
1 cup arborio rice
1 bulb fennel, halved lengthways and thinly sliced
½ cup fresh chopped parsley
½ cup freshly grated parmesan

Infuse the saffron in a tablespoon of the warm stock for 10 minutes, then return it to the rest of the stock with a few good grinds of black pepper.

Heat the oil in a large, heavy-based saucepan, add the onion and cook for 60 seconds. Add the garlic and cook for another 60 seconds, then add the rice, stirring to coat each grain with oil. Add a cup of warm stock and the sliced fennel, stirring constantly until the fennel starts to wilt. When most of the liquid has been absorbed, add the remaining stock in 3 or 4 batches. Stir frequently and make sure that each batch of the stock is fully absorbed before adding the next.

You will notice the risotto change to become thick and creamy towards the end of the cooking time. At this stage, stir in the parsley and the parmesan. Taste, and season with salt and pepper if desired. Serve immediately.

Serves 3–4

kalamata olives with fennel and basil

We are most grateful to Lucio Galleto and Timothy Fisher for allowing us to include this incredibly more-ish recipe from *The Art of Food at Lucio's* (Craftsman House, 1999).

250 g (9 oz) kalamata olives, pitted
1 fennel bulb
3 garlic cloves, peeled and slightly bruised
5 fresh basil leaves, chopped
extra virgin olive oil

Rinse the olives under running water and dry them in a salad spinner to remove all traces of water. Wash the fennel and cut it into pieces twice the size of the olives. In a large bowl, combine the olives, fennel, garlic and basil. Drizzle with olive oil and mix until all ingredients are well combined. Let stand for at least 4 hours, and remove the garlic before serving.

WILD FENNEL

This tall-growing perennial (*F. vulgare*) does not produce the swollen stem base of the annual variety. It is looked upon as something of a weed and is usually found growing wild in low-lying places that are subject to flooding and also along roadside banks and ditches. It is often wrongly referred to as aniseed because of a similarity in flavour and appearance.

fenugreek

trigonella foenum-graecum

Fenugreek is one of the oldest cultivated plants – you can read all about it in papyri from Egyptian tombs (it was used in the embalming process). Today it is commercially grown, particularly for its seeds that have a strong, spicy-yet-sweet scent and are rather bitter to the taste. The ground seeds are often included in curry spice mixes and pastes. It seems incongruous, but they are also used to make artificial maple syrup – think of that next time you smell them, and you'll detect that sweet, maple-syrup aroma beyond the initial spiciness.

Fenugreek has the ability to make itself indispensable wherever it is grown. In India, the leaves are used as a vegetable known as *methi*, as a flavouring for curries, as a key ingredient in tandoori marinades and are added torn or whole to green salads served to freshen the palate (and tone up the system). Their mild flavour goes well with potatoes and spinach.

The Iranians make a delectable and one of the easiest-ever appetisers with a variety of fresh herbs – usually fenugreek, parsley, garlic chives, tarragon, coriander, mint, and watercress. All you do is wash, dry and roughly tear the herbs, crisp them in the refrigerator, and serve them on a platter with cubes of feta and flat bread.

The sharpness of fenugreek sprouts combines well with the mild grassiness of alfalfa. Add them to sandwiches and salad with a little oil and lemon dressing.

If you have fenugreek growing, freeze the fresh leaves in ice-cube trays by chopping them finely and mixing with a little water.

GROWING

Fenugreek is a small, slender annual from the pea family (*Fabaceae*, formerly *Leguminosae*) with aromatic light green leaves about 2 cm (¾ in) long. It looks rather like alfalfa. The Romans called it *foenum-graecum* (meaning Greek hay) when they brought it to Italy, because the foliage was a fodder crop used to sweeten mildewed, sour hay.

Fenugreek grows to about 60 cm (24 in) and likes full sun and well-drained, rich, alkaline soil. Sow some seeds in spring, and more a few weeks later to stagger your crop. Make narrow furrows, plant your seeds or seedlings about 10 cm (4 in) apart, and water well. Because it is a rather delicate annual, don't try to transplant it. Just pop it straight into its permanent spot in the garden (or into a container). Pick the leaves as soon as they are large enough to add to salads.

Small, yellowish-white flowers bloom in late summer, and are followed by typical leguminous fruits in light brown, sickle-shaped seed pods about as long as your finger, about three to five months after sowing. These contain small, furrowed, golden-brown seeds that look like little pebbles with their rather square irregular shapes. When the pods are ripe, collect them as the first few seeds fall from them.

DRYING

Drying fenugreek leaves is not hard – pick sprays of the spindly leaf-bearing stems and spread them out in a thin layer on clean paper or cloth. Leave them in an airy, shady place until they're dry, or if the weather is humid, you can spread them on a baking tray and dry them in the oven. Heat the oven to about 50°C (120°F), then turn it off. Put the tray of leaves in and leave the oven door ajar. By the time the oven has cooled, the leaves should be dry – if not, repeat the whole process.

To dry the seeds, snip off the pods and hang them in bunches or spread them out on a tray in a warm dry place. When completely dry, shake the seeds from the pods and store them in labelled airtight containers.

spinach frittata with fenugreek leaves

This versatile frittata is made in minutes and is equally delicious hot or cold. Serve it with a mesclun salad.

4 eggs
2 tablespoons water
salt and pepper
pinch of chilli powder (optional)
1 cup cooked spinach leaves, roughly chopped
about 15 fresh fenugreek leaves
1 teaspoon butter

Beat the eggs and water together with the salt, pepper and chilli. Stir in the spinach and fenugreek leaves. Melt the butter in a heavy-based frying pan, tilting the pan as the butter melts to coat the surface. Pour in the egg mixture and cook over low heat, gently lifting the edges of the frittata away from the pan as they set, to allow uncooked mixture to flow down the sides. Pre-heat the grill as you continue the lifting-and-tilting action, letting the uncooked portions flow to the edges and base of the pan. When it is nearly all set, transfer the pan to the grill until the top has lightly browned and the frittata is completely cooked.

Serves 2

panch phora blend

Panch phora is one of those blends that makes a meal special, and better still, a little goes a long way. Add it to curries; fry potato cubes in olive oil and panch phora; or mix it with minced beef (about 1 tablespoon panch phora to 1 kg (2 lb) minced beef) for a tasty meat loaf or meatballs.

3 teaspoons brown mustard seeds
2½ teaspoons nigella seeds (also called kalonji or
   black onion seeds)
2 teaspoons cumin seeds
1½ teaspoons fenugreek seeds
1 teaspoon fennel seeds

Mix all the seeds together and store in an airtight container. The blend will keep for about 12 months.

Makes about ⅓ cup

garlic

allium sativum

Borage Soup (recipe page 32)

Compôte of Dates with Figs and Aniseed (recipe page 13)

Garlic's culinary virtues have been indispensable in many cuisines from East Asia to Spain for centuries, as its unique aroma heightens the taste and aroma of a dish. In fact, garlic has been known for so many thousands of years that its origins are rather obscure. It belongs to the same family (*Alliaceae*) as onions, chives and leeks, and the *Macquarie Dictionary* tells us the name we know it by today comes from the Middle English word garleac – 'gar' meaning a spear and 'leac' a leek.

There was a time not so very long ago when eating garlic in even minute quantities would put one at the receiving end of dark looks and 'you've had garlic!' accusations. How our cuisine has changed. So, what goes with garlic? Easier to ask today what doesn't!

Although the garlic-growers of California delight in putting it with jams and ice-cream, most of us would draw the line there and say you can add garlic to virtually anything that's savoury – lamb, pork, veal, beef, chicken, tomatoes, eggplant (aubergine), zucchini (courgette), curries, Asian cooking, certain sauces and dressings.

For those who feel that garlic is an acquired taste and prefer only the merest whiff, rubbing the sides of a salad bowl, or casserole dish with a cut clove may deliver the desired effect.

For the rest, there is aioli ...

This thick, strong-tasting, golden mayonnaise from rural France is made with eggs, olive oil and crushed garlic and goes with just about anything. It is delicious with steamed baby new potatoes, a bowl of shelled hard-boiled eggs, globe artichokes, avocado, asparagus, fish, chicken, or simply mopped up with chunks of baguette.

When buying bulbs of fresh garlic, look for ones that are firmly held together. The cloves should be hard and not shrinking away from each other. There are various types of garlic on the market, ranging from small Asian ones to the Californian giants. Keep bulbs intact until you need to use a clove or few, and store in an open container like a wicker basket in a cool, airy place (not the refrigerator as the bulbs tend to sprout in damp conditions). So long as they have their protective husk the bulbs don't smell – that only emerges when you crush or peel the cloves.

There is also a single clove type of garlic, about the size of a golf ball, that has been grown in the high, cold areas of China for centuries. The Japanese love its extra hot and pungent flavour used raw. When cooked, the flavour is milder than our more familiar garlic and it makes a fantastic baked vegetable. It's peeled just like onion, and with the outside rather caramelised and the inside cooked to creamy perfection, it is a mouth-watering delight.

Should garlic be chopped, crushed or sliced? It's a matter of taste – encountering a slice of well-cooked garlic in a hearty beef casserole is a delight to any garlic-lover, while a fine purée of crushed garlic cloves is perfect for a curry paste.

Or you can try this: slice the top off an entire bulb of garlic, just low enough to cut the tops off the cloves, then cook in the oven or on the barbecue until the garlic flesh is soft and creamy. Squeeze the flesh out of the papery shells, and enjoy this delectable taste sensation that has none of the pungency of raw garlic.

You can buy garlic ready prepared, as peeled cloves, paste or dried. Store peeled cloves and pastes in the refrigerator once opened and dried garlic products in their airtight pack in a cupboard. Don't buy garlic powder if it looks lumpy as this may reveal telltale signs of extra moisture – meaning that it simply won't pack the necessary punch.

GROWING

Garlic grows to about 90 cm (36 in) high and has flat, greyish leaves about 30 cm (12 in) long, a bit like a nondescript lily. However there's nothing nondescript about the fabulous flower, which appears in summer. A willowy, round, flower stalk thrusts upward from the centre above the leaves and produces a typical allium pompom flower – a blossomy ball of mauve-tinted white petals sometimes used in arrangements by imaginative florists.

Spring is the best time for planting garlic. Mature bulbs are made up of tightly clustered cloves, each sheathed in a pearly, papery skin. The whole bulb is tissue-wrapped by nature in the same covering. Separate the cloves (but don't peel them) and, press them upright with the root end pointing down, in pre-dug holes 5 cm (2 in) deep. The root end is the one with the tough, flat, button-sized base. Plant the cloves about 15 cm (6 in) apart in a sunny spot in the garden or in a container in rich, well-dug and well-drained soil. If the soil is poor, dig in some well-decayed manure or compost. Cover the cloves with soil, and water well.

Soon the spear-like, grey-green leaves appear, followed by the flower stalks, each with a long, swelling bud at the end. As the stalks lengthen and the buds grow plumper, they eventually burst into flower. Harvesting usually takes place about six months after planting the cloves, when the flowers are fading and the leaves are yellowing and beginning to shrivel. You can plant garlic seeds, but the results are very erratic as many are infertile. In cooler districts the bulbs are likely to be smaller.

DRYING

Pull the whole plant out by hand after loosening the roots first. Remove the excess soil by tapping the bulbs against the spade or your boot. Trim off the roots with garden shears and leave the tops intact so that the sap will move down into the corms (bulbs). Leave the bulbs in a shady place for about a week to toughen up the skin, then cut away any foliage and store in a dry airy container such as a basket. Bulbs should keep for around four months. You can also plait several bulbs together with the remaining leaves and hang them in a dry place where air is circulating. In a moist atmosphere the bulbs will mildew.

aioli with lemon myrtle

12 cloves garlic, peeled

1 teaspoon salt

3 egg yolks

1¾ cups extra virgin olive oil

a few drops of lemon juice

1 teaspoon dried and crushed lemon myrtle leaves

Chop the garlic cloves very finely to a thick paste consistency, then transfer to a bowl. Add the salt and the egg yolks, stirring with a wooden spoon, until well blended. At this stage, swap your wooden spoon for a wire whisk and beat in the olive oil drop by drop. As the mixture thickens, and when about half the oil has been used, pour the rest of the oil a little more quickly, in a steady stream, still beating. Finally, add the lemon juice and lemon myrtle.

If the oil separates, put a fresh egg yolk in another bowl and slowly add the curdled sauce to it, beating constantly.

Makes about 2 cups

horseradish

armoracia rusticana

It is white and rather like a radish, but is hairier and more wrinkled, has a faithful following, and can clear your sinuses in a whiff. It is horseradish, a member of the sulfurous mustard and cress family (*Cruciferae*). Its root system comprises a main or taproot, about 30 cm (12 in) long and 1.25 cm (½ in) thick, with several smaller roots branching out at various angles.

Like so many herbs, horseradish has been valued for so long no-one knows quite where it came from originally. But finely sliced rare roast beef cries out for it. Horseradish combined with vinegar was a favourite condiment in Germany and its reputation spread from there to England and France, where it became known as *moutarde des Allemands*. A little freshly grated horseradish adds zest to dips, sauces and dressings and is the perfect partner for beef, pork, oily fish, and poultry. It is also good added to coleslaw, or pickled beetroot.

Horseradish is best eaten cold as it loses its piquancy when cooked because its volatile oil evaporates quickly. Grating releases the volatile oil. However, only grate the outer section of the root because that packs the pungency. The inner core tends to be on the flavourless, rubbery side.

Fresh horseradish roots are not readily available unless you grow them yourself, or live in a major city with a Chinatown area, where you can find them if you're lucky. You can buy jars of horseradish relish or paste and grated fresh horseradish root these days (refrigerate after opening), but they're quite a bit milder than the freshly grated root.

Dehydrated horseradish granules or flakes are convenient to use when making sauces and dressings. Store in airtight packs in a cupboard away from heat and light to preserve the flavour. When these are reconstituted, the chunky pieces can be a bit leathery –

keep them covered with water for about 24 hours, adding more as it is absorbed. Then purée them in a blender to make a paste and store it in a covered container in the fridge until you need it.

The young leaves can be added to salads, but their flavour and texture is rather coarse, so it's no wonder that, more often than not, they're passed over in favour of more pleasing salad herbs such as salad burnet, mitsuba, chicory, purslane and sorrel.

Japanese horseradish (*wasabi*) is from a different plant (*Wasabia*) but packs an equivalent punch, and is the key to the popularity of sushi and sashimi.

GROWING

Perennial horseradish is easily grown in temperate zones in rich, loose, moist soil in sun or light shady conditions. 'Easy to grow' is an understatement. It is such a vigorous grower that even the most dedicated devotees should possibly think twice before planting. Its large, dark green spinach-like leaves are soft and fleshy, and constantly under attack by leaf-eating pests, particularly snails.

If you want to grow horseradish in your garden, give it plenty of room, allowing about 30 cm (12 in) between plants all round. Unless you have a remote corner of your garden where your horseradish can reign supreme, it might be wise to restrict it to a large tub, planting it in a nice sandy loam. In early spring, select your taproots, cut off any side roots and plant in prepared holes about 20 cm (8 in) long and 2.5 cm (1 in) wide, pouring a little sand around the sides before covering with soil. Keep watered so that the roots don't become coarse.

To encourage root development, the panicles of white flowers that develop in summer are usually cut back, which is no great loss, as horseradish doesn't usually set seed. Propagate by dividing an established clump, although this is seldom necessary, because once you have it, you have it for life.

Dig up roots in autumn or as needed. You only use the small side roots in cooking, not the main taproot, which can be replanted as described above. Scrape the soil away from the side of the plant, and cut the small roots away. Every two years, pull the whole plant out, keeping the taproots for propagation. Store the side roots in dry sand or wash them well and preserve them whole or sliced in white wine vinegar.

horseradish sauce

For roast beef, pork or lamb.

200 ml (7 fl oz) sour cream
1/2 tablespoon white vinegar
1 teaspoon mustard powder
1/2 teaspoon salt
1 teaspoon sugar
2 tablespoons fresh grated horseradish or 1 tablespoon
    dried horseradish, reconstituted in warm water

Whip the cream until thickened, and stir in all the other ingredients. Let stand for at least 30 minutes before serving. Store in the refrigerator and use within 3 or 4 days.

Makes about 1 cup

apple, mint and horseradish cream

Combined with mint and apples, horseradish adds a zing to vegetables like avocado, beetroot and cucumber and also to sashimi.

2 Granny Smith or other cooking apples
2 tablespoons freshly grated horseradish
juice of 1 lemon
1 teaspoon salt
1 teaspoon sugar
2 teaspoons chopped fresh mint
200 ml (7 fl oz) sour cream

Peel and grate the apples and combine with all the other ingredients. Store in a covered container in the refrigerator and use within 3 or 4 days.

Makes about 1 cup

hyssop

hyssopus officinalis

Go easy with this one in your cooking, though it's a lovely plant to have in your garden. Hyssop's leaves have a curious musky aroma and a palate-tingling flavour of Angostura bitters, so judicious use is, well, judicious. Used sparingly, though, its distinctive aroma never intrudes, but rather enhances. This herb has an intriguing, pungent, pine flavour that combines well with fatty meats like duck, pork, or goose and it can also be added to stuffings for these meats. In this way, we could consider it the herb equivalent of spicy juniper berries. Stir a few chopped leaves into a rich gravy or sprinkle into soup during the last half-hour of cooking. The delightfully scented, rich blue flowers colour a green salad. But you will have to grow your own as it's not available through fruit and vegetable retailers.

Hyssop was a holy herb used for purification rites in temples. Monastery gardens were planted with hyssop for religious, medicinal and landscaping purposes – the good monks found its bushy habit and sapphire flowers useful for outlining their cloistered, formal herb beds.

This particularly useful plant provided not only culinary delights, but also aromatic oil for perfumes and medicines for all sorts of medieval mishaps, from acne to worms. Even today, the leaves, flowers and stems are distilled to produce a fine, colourless oil used in manufacturing perfumes and liqueurs.

GROWING

Hyssop can be mistaken for winter savory until it flowers in late summer: both carry spires of small, lipped blooms in late summer and early autumn. However, winter savory's flowers are white, while hyssop's, which are full of nectar and loved by bees, are deep blue – except for some scarcer pink or white varieties. Like savory, hyssop draws back into itself in winter, looking squat, and its leaves dark green and unyielding. Come spring, up shoot the tender green shoots on lengthening stalks and this is when it is hard to tell them apart.

Hyssop is a densely compact perennial growing to about 60 cm (24 in), making it excellent for low hedges (remember the good monks). It is also suitable for container planting. It's easy to grow, either by root division (in spring or autumn), from cuttings (in late spring to early summer), or from seed (in the spring). When planting out, choose a sunny spot and light well-drained soil. If you're growing hyssop as a low hedge, set seedlings about 30 cm (12 in) apart. It is frost-hardy and, thanks to its Mediterranean origins, happy in dry conditions. Prune stalks and stems back to the main plant in autumn, which will assure its shape and vigour for the following spring.

DRYING

Dried hyssop flowers are used extensively in herbal medicine, and are harvested during peak blossoming time in late summer. Cut flowering stems in the morning and hang in bunches in a dry, shady place, or spread out on sheet of paper or one drying racks. When dry and moisture-free, strip the flowers and some leaves from their stalks and store in airtight, labelled containers.

honeyed carrot straws with hyssop

2 medium carrots, cut into julienne strips
1 tablespoon water
1 teaspoon honey
1 teaspoon finely chopped hyssop
salt and pepper to taste

Place all the ingredients in a heavy-based saucepan, cover and simmer slowly for about 10 minutes, depending on the size of your carrot pieces. Serve hot.

Serves 2–3 as an accompaniment

raw cauliflower and hyssop salad

This recipe is for those weeks when cauliflower is at premium freshness.

2–3 cups cauliflower florets
1 apple, chopped into small dice
1 tablespoon finely chopped hyssop
2 teaspoons salt
2 cups plain yoghurt
1 tablespoon lemon juice

Slice the florets paper-thin lengthwise, and mix with the chopped apple in a bowl. Add the hyssop, salt, yoghurt and lemon juice, mix well and chill. A couple of fresh hyssop sprigs will add panache to the presentation.

Serves 4 as an accompaniment

kaffir lime tree

citrus hystrix

The fresh leaves of this delightful smelling but ferociously thorny tree are used extensively in Asian cooking – in sambals, with steamed fish, in the beef rendang of Indonesia, in laksa, green curries, soups and many dishes made with coconut cream. They add a fresh nuance to chicken soup or any spicy fish dish. Lemon leaves, or leaves from West Indian and Tahitian limes, are sometimes substituted. For maximum freshness and flavour, the leaves are best straight from the tree. They are usually removed from a dish before serving.

The kaffir lime is a typical evergreen citrus tree with dark green, smooth leaves that are long, flat, and deliciously lime-scented. What makes them different is the unusual double leaf, which looks as though a whole new leaf has grown out of the end of the original leaf. Botanists will tell you that the original leaf is in fact just a very large nodule from which the real leaf grows, but to us lay persons, the important thing is that we get twice as much leaf! The aromatic foliage is high in volatile oils, which give the leaves their unique flavour.

Not only are the leaves perfect in the pot, but you can also crush a few and place them in a small glass dish as a natural room deodoriser. They emit a heavenly scent that's a cross between lemon, orange and lime, but not like any one of these on its own.

You don't have to grow your own. You can buy fresh leaves from fruit and vegetable retailers, Asian food shops and produce markets. If you do have a tree, pick your own fresh lime leaves as needed, watching out for the prickles. You can freeze fresh leaves in a plastic bag (it helps them keep their flavour) and simply add the frozen leaves straight to the dish; there's no need to thaw them first.

GROWING

Kaffir lime trees thrive in tropical and sub-tropical climes, and even in temperate zones in full sun in warmer areas. As the branches have large prickles, plant the trees away from where children play. You can also grow them very satisfactorily in large pots. And if your pot can be wheeled around, you can follow the sun. In summer, the white, fragrant flowers come into bloom, followed by small green limes with a rough, bumpy surface that contain very little juice.

As kaffir limes trees are grafted, buy them ready to plant from the nursery. Plant in light, deep, well-drained soil in a sunny, frost-free position. They are tropical, surface-rooting trees, and need mulching to prevent evaporation of moisture from the soil, especially in dry weather. Keep them weed free and give the tree a good soaking in dry weather, rather than watering lightly. Prune away dead wood, being careful of the long thorns.

As citrus trees are ravenous feeders, an annual application of some good fertiliser is essential in spring. Be careful cultivating near the surface so as not to injure or cut the fine, shallow roots. By fertilising and cultivating regularly as the tree grows, the roots are encouraged downwards and are in better condition to resist dry, hot weather. If your tree is in a tub, remember that it is depending on you for all its nutrients, and you will need to feed it more often.

Pests and diseases like aphids, ants, lace bug and scale can be a problem, as with all citrus. As it is the leaves you eat, opt for a minimum chemical cure, or look for a treatment formulated for vegetables. Try soapy water for the aphids, white oil for the scale and learn to live with the ants.

DRYING

The leaves dry well if you take a little care. You can hang them in bunches like bay leaves, and use them in varying degrees of dryness. But for best results, spread freshly picked leaves out on porous paper in a single layer in a warm, dark place where humidity is low. Store crisp, dried leaves in airtight containers away from light, extreme heat and humidity and they will last about 12 months. The dry leaves should be green, not yellow.

coconut rice

2 cups basmati rice

1 cup water

1 cup coconut milk

1 stalk lemongrass, finely chopped

Put the rice into a saucepan with the water, coconut milk and lemongrass. Cover the pan and bring to a boil over a medium heat. Once the rice is boiling, turn off the heat and allow to steam for 15 minutes.

Serves 4

beef stir-fry with kaffir lime

1 tablespoon sesame oil

300 g (10 oz) sirloin steak, sliced

5 red shallots, sliced

2 cloves garlic, finely chopped

2 long red chillis, sliced

3 kaffir lime leaves, sliced into julienne strips

1 cup sugar snap peas

1 tablespoon soy sauce

2 teaspoons fish sauce

2 cups Thai basil

Heat the sesame oil in a wok. Add the beef and stir-fry for 2–3 minutes. Add all the remaining ingredients, except for the Thai basil, and stir-fry for another 3–4 minutes. Turn off the heat and add the Thai basil to the wok. Stir it through until just wilted and serve immediately with coconut rice.

Serves 4

gyoza with kaffir lime leaf

The remaining wonton wrappers can be frozen and used later.

12 round wonton wrappers
3 tablespoons vegetable oil
½ cup water

Stuffing
150 g (5 oz) pork mince
2 kaffir lime leaves, cut into strips
1 long red chilli
1 cm (½ in) fresh ginger, chopped
1 cup chopped white cabbage
1 tablespoon soy sauce
1 teaspoon sesame oil
1 teaspoon fish sauce

Dipping Sauce
2 tablespoons soy sauce
1 long red chilli, sliced, seeds intact

Place all the stuffing ingredients in a food processor and pulse until they are well combined and form a smooth paste.

Place a generous teaspoon of stuffing into the centre of each wonton wrapper. Lightly brush around the edges of each wonton wrapper with water. Bring the edges together and pinch to seal firmly, forming a crescent shape with a flat base. Once made, the gyoza can be covered and refrigerated until ready to cook.

Heat the vegetable oil in frying pan and when hot, add the gyoza, flat side down. Fry for 2–3 minutes, or until the undersides are golden-brown. Add the water and cover the pan with a lid so the gyoza can steam. Reduce the heat and cook for 3–4 minutes. When cooked, the dumpling wrappers will appear soft and translucent.

Stir together the soy sauce and sliced chilli and serve with the gyoza.

Makes 12

lavender

lavandula

The familiar pungency of lavender usually reminds us of Grandma's linen cupboard rather than her kitchen. However, a few centuries ago, sweet-scented flowers were often used in cooking. 'W. M.' (cook to Queen Henrietta Maria in 1635) had a recipe for a conserve of lavender flowers that consisted of lavender petals finely chopped then mixed with icing sugar and enough rosewater to make a thin paste. It was then spread as a fragrant icing on plain cakes and biscuits. Lavender is also used in *herbes de Provence*, and in the exotic Moroccan mixture, *ras el hanout*.

These highly perfumed plants of the labiate or mint family are found naturally in the Mediterranean region right through the Middle East and south to India; and today are grown and loved around the world. There are about 25 species and numerous hybrids and, as the common names can vary from country to country, plant nursery to plant nursery and gardening guide to gardening guide, we recommend sticking to the botanical name when talking about this herb.

L. angustifolia, the variety we call English lavender, was not actually cultivated in England until about 1568. Today, flower colours available in hybrids of this beautiful variety range from snow white, dusty pink and shades of blue, and go through the spectrum of mauves from pale lavender to deepest purple.

Other favourites are *L. dentata* (known as French lavender or fringe lavender) and *L. stoechas* (also known as French, Italian and Spanish lavender).

L. allardii (giant lavender) is a hardy and successful hybrid; it is larger than most lavenders and has the long flower spikes and smooth leaves of *L. angustifolia*, while the foliage has the indented edges of *L. dentata*.

L. angustifolia seems to be everyone's favourite and is the one that's very popular for lavender handcrafts thanks to its highly perfumed flowers and long, elegant, leafless stalk below the bloom. Make lavender vinegar by infusing whole stems with their flowers in white vinegar for several weeks. Use it for a dressing with a green leaf and flower salad featuring nasturtium petals, heartsease flowers, marigold petals and lavender.

GROWING

When lavenders are in a position they like, the difference in the size of the bushes and the depth of colour in the flowers is very marked.

L. angustifolia is a bushy, small shrub growing 90 cm (36 in) high in the right place, with silvery, smooth, pointed leaves and highly perfumed, tiny mauve flowers at the end of long, spiky stems. Although each individual flower is indeed tiny, there are lots of them all grouped together, so that the flower head is about the diameter of a pencil, and somewhere between 2 and 4 cm ($^3/_4$–$1^1/_2$ in) long. When the bush starts blooming in summer it is a beautiful sight, especially if several plants are massed together as a hedge. This type of planting suits all the lavenders.

L. dentata is the hardiest, and in many ways the most rewarding of the varieties to grow and we have seen it reach a height of 1.5 metres (5 feet). The bush blooms continuously for about nine months of the year, especially if mature flower stalks are cut back regularly to where two new shoots are beginning to branch. This helps to keep the bush a good shape while preventing it from having to nourish flowers that are past their peak.

Lavender can be propagated from seed, but as many lavender plants available today are hybrids, taking cuttings is a much safer and quicker option. (If you try planting seeds from a hybrid lavender, the new plants will probably revert back to the original type.) Plant seeds in spring, preferably in seed boxes or trays made from bio-degradable egg cartons, with just a light dusting of soil patted down on top of the seeds. Tip cuttings of any variety should be taken in late spring when the soft, new leaves are firm enough not to wilt when they are put into a pot of sand.

When the seedlings are big enough, or when the cuttings have made roots, plant them out in a sunny, well-drained position. This is very important for lavender, as it will not grow sturdily nor flower well, if you plant it in a shady or damp place. When the plants have finished flowering, prune them hard, but not to ground level, and if you have an open fireplace, save the branches for the fire.

DRYING

The best time to pick and dry *L. angustifolia* is before the last flowers on each stalk are fully opened. This is when their oil content, and therefore their fragrance, is greatest. Pick the stems on a dry day before the heat of the sun has drawn out the volatile essence, then tie them in bunches and hang in a shady, airy place to dry. When they're really dry, strip the flowers from the stems and store them in airtight, labelled containers.

Leafy and flowering stems of *L dentata* may be cut at any time for drying, providing there is no moisture in the air and harvesting is done before midday. The benefit with *L. dentata* is that the leaves are as fragrant as the flowers, so you can achieve much more bulk by using the dried leaves as well. Hang the stalks in bunches in a shady, airy place to dry. When they're really dry, store the flowers and leaves in airtight, labelled containers.

herbes de provence

Add herbes de Provence to casseroles or cassoulet, allowing about 1 tablespoon per kilo (2 lb) of meat.

4 teaspoons dried thyme
2 teaspoons each dried marjoram and parsley
1 teaspoon dried tarragon
$2/3$ teaspoon dried lavender flowers
$1/2$ teaspoon celery seeds
1 bay leaf, crushed

Combine all the ingredients and store in an airtight container.

Makes about $1/4$ cup

Witloof Stuffed with Pork and Prawns (recipe page 45)

Top to bottom:
Native Pepperberries; Herbes de Provence (recipe page 88);
Mountain Pepperleaf Blends (recipe page 114);
Panch Phora Blend (reicpe page 71)

lavender ice-cream

2 tablespoons white dessert wine

2 tablespoons finely chopped fresh lavender leaves

2 cups thick cream

100 g (3½ oz) caster (superfine) sugar

2 egg whites

2 tablespoons fresh or dried lavender flowers

Warm the wine gently and infuse the leaves for 15–20 minutes. Strain and discard the leaves. Beat the cream until stiff and gradually mix in the wine and half the sugar. Whisk the egg whites until stiff, and whisk in the remaining sugar. Fold the meringue mixture into the cream with the lavender flowers. Spoon into a container and freeze, or use an ice-cream maker if you have one.

Serves 4

lavender potpourri

This potpourri is perfect for scented sachets or coathangers, or left in an open bowl to freshen the room. After about 6 months, gently stir through a few more drops of lavender oil with your fingers.

1 cup dried English lavender flowers

½ cup dried marjoram leaves

½ cup dried rose petals

1 tablespoon dried mint

1 tablespoon orris root powder

2 teaspoons ground coriander seed

½ teaspoon ground cloves

a few drops lavender oil

Mix the flowers and leaves together. Blend the orris root powder, coriander and cloves, then stir in the lavender oil and add to the dried ingredients. Stir well to combine.

IF LAVENDER IS THE QUEEN OF HERBS, SWEET CICELY IS SURELY THE PRINCESS . . .

Sweet cicely (*Myrrhis odorata*), one of the tall, stately herbs – reaching 60–150 cm (24–60 in) in the right position – is covered with a froth of white flower umbels in the spring, much to the delight of the bee population. This charming plant has ferny foliage with a sweet, warm, anise taste and thick, hollow and branching stems, similar to those of angelica. It has also been called fern-leaved chervil or giant sweet chervil, although it is a much bigger plant in every way than the real chervil. Most parts of sweet cicely are edible. The leaves, green seeds and stems can be chopped and used in all kinds of salads. The hollow stems may also be candied like angelica. The finely chopped leaves are excellent to use when cooking sharp fruit like rhubarb to counteract acidity, and, although not as sweet as stevia, the leaves will bring a natural sweetness to cooling summer drinks.

lemongrass

cymbopogon citratus

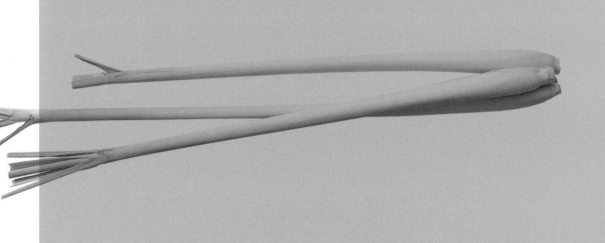

Lemongrass is a great multiplier, growing in bushy clumps about 90 cm (36 in) tall that increase in girth with each passing year. Its long, narrow, lemon-scented leaves bend gracefully outwards and have a slightly sticky texture. Watch out, the edges are razor sharp. Usually a pale yellowish-green, at certain times of the year the leaves are rust coloured at the tips. The bulbous lower stem is an essential ingredient in South-East Asian cooking where it is used whole or finely sliced in curries, soups, salads and Thai curry pastes.

One reason it is so popular in Asian recipes is that the stem is packed with citral, the substance found in the outer rind of lemons – lemons themselves don't grow well in the tropics. Lemongrass is delicious with steamed seafood and poultry dishes, marinades for pork, and whole fish barbecued in foil.

The leaves aren't often used in cooking, but try snipping a few fresh pieces of leaf into a pot of tea for a refreshing, lemony flavour, or adding to the water when poaching fish or chicken.

Lemongrass is a very fibrous plant so there are some tricks of the trade to using it. Peel away the tough, outer layers and finely slice the pale lower stem crosswise so that there are no long fibres to spoil the texture of your finished dish. The electric blender comes to the rescue if you need to pound or grind the sliced stem to make a paste. Tie a couple of complete stems into a knot, bruise lightly with a rolling pin, and drop it whole into soups or sauces, so that it is easy to lift out before serving.

If you are buying lemongrass, avoid dry stems and pick out ones that are firm and white, with the slightest hint of a greenish tinge. Excess stems can be bruised and used whole or cut into slices. Wrap in plastic and store in the freezer for up to six months. Our old friend Bernard King freezes the stalks, then uses kitchen scissors to snip lengthways at one end to make a little brush. He then uses this to brush his marinade over barbecued chicken and fish.

GROWING

In temperate zones, perennial lemongrass will grow easily year round. However it does not like dry conditions (remember, it is from the tropics), and flourishes best in rich, moist soil in a sheltered position in the garden where it can bask in morning sun. If your winters are cold and frosty, lift the plants in mid-autumn, pot them using a good soil mixture and keep indoors until spring, when you can plant them back into the garden.

Lemongrass grows to about a metre (around 3 feet) high. If your clump is losing its attractive, bushy appearance and becoming too spindly and straggly, cut about 15 cm (6 in) off the tops of the leaves. Frequent cutting is good for the plant, so chop away and use it with gay abandon in your cooking.

In spring, the old leaves should be cut down to where the new shoots are appearing, then divide the roots by digging well down into the ground with a spade, cutting cleanly through the main bush and taking as many clumps as you can without damaging the parent plant. Put the new shoots into prepared ground immediately, firm down the soil and water well. In mild areas the clump may be cut through and divided in the same way at any time of the year. In autumn, when the grassy clump is thick and green, cut the leaves back to within a couple of inches of the base.

DRYING

Dry leaves by hanging them in bunches in a shady, airy place, or spreading them out on racks or on clean newspaper. As the leaves are full of etheric oils, they will dry quickly. Cut them with scissors into short lengths and put into clean, dry, airtight containers.

vietnamese chicken with lemongrass

Lemongrass lends its own special character to many dishes, however we couldn't go past one of our all-time favourites from Charmaine Solomon's *The Complete Asian Cookbook* (New Holland, 2002).

1 small roasting chicken, about 1 kg (2 lb)

3 or 4 stalks lemongrass

3 spring onions (scallions)

1 teaspoon salt

¼ teaspoon black pepper, plus extra to taste

2 tablespoons oil

1 or 2 fresh red chillies, seeded and chopped

2 teaspoons sugar

½ cup roasted peanuts, finely chopped

2 tablespoons fish sauce

Cut chicken into small serving pieces, Chinese style, chopping through bones with a cleaver. Remove the outer leaves of lemongrass and finely slice the tender white part at the base of the stalks. Bruise with mortar and pestle. Finely slice the spring onions, including the green leaves. Mix the chicken with the salt, pepper, lemongrass and spring onions and set aside for 30 minutes.

Heat a wok, add oil and when oil is hot add chicken mixture and stir-fry for 3 minutes. Add the chillies and stir-fry on medium heat for a further 10 minutes or until the chicken no longer looks pink. Season with sugar and extra black pepper and add the peanuts. Stir well. Add the fish sauce and toss to distribute evenly, then serve with rice or noodles.

Serves 4

lemon myrtle

backhousia citriodora

Lemon myrtle is probably the best known and most loved of the Australian native plants that have been accepted as herbs and spices. As the name suggests, the flavour of the leaves is intensely lemony, with suggestions of lemon verbena, lime and lemongrass. Like many other native herbs, the flavour of the leaves can be lost in long cooking, so it's best to use them in an infusion where they can be lifted out, like bay leaves. For example, warm the leaves with milk for a custard or ice-cream – the heat will be sufficient to release the flavour but not destroy the volatile oils responsible for the flavour.

Lemon myrtle complements chicken, vegetable and seafood stir-fries and is a good substitute for lemongrass. Try sprinkling a little on meat, chicken or fish before grilling or barbecuing. And if you have a sore throat, it makes a deliciously soothing lemony tea.

If you have a tree, pick the more intensely flavoured darker, mature leaves as you need them. You can sometimes buy fresh leaves from specialty Australian native foods suppliers; however dried whole or powdered leaves, which have a more intense flavour than the fresh, are usually readily available from gourmet herb and spice outlets. Because lemon myrtle's essential oil is so volatile, it's best to buy in small quantities – say 10 g (1/2 oz) at a time.

The history of this herb is proudly Australian, though there are now plantations in many other parts of the world, and they are growing trees for oil extraction in parts of southern Asia. Lemon myrtle's citral content – the component identified as the lemon flavour – is about 90 per cent; compared with around 80 per cent in lemongrass and only 6 per cent in lemons. So it's understandable that the food industry is interested in harvesting this intense flavour (without any citrus acidity) for food manufacture and processing in products ranging from yoghurt and ice-cream, to biscuits and breads, and sauces and syrups.

GROWING

Lemon myrtle reaches about 20 metres (66 feet) in its native Queensland rainforests, and about 8 metres (26 feet) in more southern, frost-free areas. Because of its rather shrubby shape, it makes a very ornamental native addition to the garden, and is especially useful for filling up a corner or hiding a wall.

Trees are readily available from native plant nurseries in Australia. When not influenced by us humans, they propagate from seed; but we are impatient by nature and have found that cuttings strike quite easily. Take cuttings about 20 cm (8 in) long from branches with a pencil-sized diameter, trimming the leaves from the lower end. Plant the cuttings about

7.5–10 cm (3–4 in) deep in good river sand or potting mixture in a pot with a top diameter of about 10 cm (4 in). Keep watered until you can see roots appearing in the drainage holes in the pot, then transfer to a larger pot. Let it grow on in a bucket-sized pot in a sunny spot until it's about 50 cm (20 in) tall and the roots are well established.

Now's the time to plant your lemon myrtle in its permanent spot in the garden in deep rich soil. Once established, it is quite hardy and will be happy so long as it gets at least 2–3 hours sun a day.

DRYING

Choose mature leaves as they have more flavour than the young ones. In addition, if you pick the young leaves, the tree won t look as lovely in the garden and will have nothing left to grow to maturity. Dry the leaves on a rack in a cool, airy, dark place, and store in an airtight, labelled container for later use.

tuna steaks with lemon myrtle

This mixture of lemon myrtle and salt can also be rubbed over the skin of a chicken before roasting. When a few extra lemon myrtle leaves are stuffed into the cavity with a wedge of lemon and a couple of cloves of garlic, the smell is heavenly.

½ teaspoon ground dried lemon myrtle, or 2 fresh leaves, shredded finely
½ teaspoon flaky salt
2 pieces of boneless tuna
a good quality olive oil spray

Mix the lemon myrtle and salt together, and rub over both sides of the tuna. Spray the tuna lightly with olive oil and leave to stand for about 10 minutes. Heat a heavy-based pan, spray with oil, and cook the tuna for 2–3 minutes on each side, or a little longer if you like your fish well done. Serve immediately.

Serves 2

lemon verbena

aloysia triphylla (formerly lippia citriodora)

The fragrance of lemon verbena always reminds me of our early married years and the countless sleep pillows I made using dried lemon verbena for sweet dreams, lavender for sound sleep and rose petals to wake refreshed. There was a double row of these small deciduous trees growing in the Somerset Cottage herb garden, and in summer, the pale, hazy pinky-mauve flowerets clustered in scented plumes at the tips of their leafy branches.

During spring, summer, and autumn, lemon verbena is covered profusely with pointed leaves of light green, about 10 cm (4 in) long, with a slightly sticky feel owing to their rich oil-bearing properties. I used to pick boxes and boxes of the long branches, preferably without flowers, and strip the leaves from them until my fingers were stained green. Their perfume is strong and easily released, even by merely brushing past the foliage, which immediately fills the air with a delicious lemony fragrance.

A traditional use for lemon verbena leaves was to float them in finger bowls at banquets. In a more domestic setting, however, two or three fresh lemon verbena leaves placed on top of a rice pudding or baked custard before it goes into the oven impart a delicate flavour. In the same manner, a few leaves arranged on the bottom of a buttered cake tin before the mixture is spooned in, release their aromatic oils while the cake is baking; they can be peeled off when the cake has cooled. This is particularly delicious with chocolate cakes.

Ever the experimenter, I once thought to use lemon verbena-infused rainwater for my iron, imagining the divine scent it would impart – it didn't work, proving that even with something so strongly aromatic, there are limits.

Because the dried leaves retain their flavour so effectively, lemon verbena is a must in the mix for potpourri and many fragrant gifts. The fresh leaves can also be added whole to Asian clear soups and stocks in the same way as lemon myrtle. Treat them like bay leaves and remove them after cooking. However, if you want to use fresh lemon verbena leaves, you'll probably have to grow your own tree. The leaves are rarely available fresh; and dried you are more likely to come across them inside fragrant gifts in craft shops or blended with herbal tea mixes.

GROWING

Plant your lemon verbena tree in a sheltered, sunny position where the soil is medium to light and well drained. During hot summers, mulch the roots with leaf mould or grass cuttings and water well; later, the roots will also need mulching to protect them from frost. When the tree is about three years old, you need to prune it, either in autumn or early winter, otherwise it will get too leggy. When it's pruned regularly, the tree will reward you by growing thicker and taller every year, to an eventual height of about 2 metres (6½ feet).

Young trees are readily available from major garden nurseries. You can also propagate from hardwood cuttings in late winter. Divide the wood into 15 cm (6 in) pieces, trim off any side shoots, and press each piece into a deep pot of river sand, leaving one-third of the wood exposed at the top, and water well. When the cuttings have made strong roots, plant them out into the garden. Tip cuttings are taken in late spring to early summer; trim the stems of foliage, allowing several leaves to remain at the top, then insert into the sand and continue in the same way as described for hardwood propagation.

For harvesting the leaves, cut the branches before midday, particularly during the vigorous growing seasons of summer and early autumn. Flowers on the boughs are an excellent addition with the leaves to potpourri.

Remember, lemon verbena is a deciduous tree, so as winter approaches the leaves will begin to turn yellow and fall, until, by mid-winter, the branches are quite bare.

DRYING

You can dry the leaves quickly and easily by tying cut branches together and hanging them in a cool, shady, airy place. When they're dry, strip off all the foliage and store in airtight containers. However, there are hazards in this method, as you'll also strip the skin from your fingers on the brittle leaf-stems.

By stripping the fresh green leaves from the branches before drying, you're rewarded with a luscious pile of fragrant foliage that can be spread out on sheets of newspaper, or better still, onto fly-screens raised up on a few bricks. I used to wish I could dive into them the way Scrooge McDuck dived into his money bin! The dried leaves should be dark-green, crisp and lemon scented. They should not smell musty.

fresh and zingy chicken broth

1 chicken carcase (available from poultry shops and some
    delicatessens) or 1 chicken with legs, wings and
    breast removed
1 onion, peeled and quartered
3 cm (1½ in) fresh ginger, peeled and finely chopped
2 cloves garlic, finely chopped
½ teaspoon ground nutmeg
juice and grated zest of 1 lemon
1 carrot, scraped and chopped
3 cups water
a sprig of Vietnamese mint (about 12 leaves)
a sprig of lemon verbena (about 20 fresh leaves, or
    12 dried leaves)
salt and pepper to taste

Place all the ingredients in a large saucepan and bring to the boil. Cover, reduce the heat, and simmer very gently for 45 minutes, or until the chicken flesh falls from the bones. The longer and slower the cooking, the more flavour you will extract from the chicken bones. For the last 5 minutes of the cooking time, remove the lid and increase the heat so that the stock reduces a little. Remove the carcase and bones and skim off leaves before serving the broth with its delicious vegetables and aromatics.

Serves 2–3

lovage

levisticum officinale

Lovage looks rather like a sparse version of angelica, although it does not grow as tall or as densely and has smaller, sulphur-yellow flowers borne in delicate umbels rather than great round heads. The slim stems bear flat, serrated, dark, green leaves in threes branching out from thicker, channelled stalks.

You could almost say, in a Russian-doll kind of way, that Italian parsley is a small version of lovage, which in turn is a small version of angelica. The flavour of the leaves is a combination of celery and parsley, but predominantly celery, with an extra peppery bite. When they're young, the plants also look like a rather obscure herb called smallage, said to be the forerunner of our modern celery.

People on a salt-free diet like lovage for its spicy peppery taste, and since we opened Herbie's Spices, we've often had customers looking for this herb for medieval-style banquets.

The fresh leaves are really excellent in soups and stocks, and they complement omelettes, scrambled eggs and mashed potato, just chopped and sprinkled on top. Chop the leaves finely for best results, as they are a little coarse. The hollow stalks and stems can be preserved as a confection in the same way as angelica.

The popularity of peppery lovage leaves has waned since its medieval heyday, which is why you won't find it in fruit and vegetable retailers. If you want it you'll probably have to grow it. Pick and use the leaves fresh throughout the spring and summer or freeze for when you need them by the ice-cube method. Whole leaf sprays may be stored for several weeks in the freezer by sealing them in foil.

Stems can be cut and used at any time. If you're candying them like angelica stems, the flavour is best just after flowering.

GROWING

Like angelica, perennial lovage likes rich, moist soil and a rather shady spot to grow well. Plant seedlings or sow seeds in the spring, directly into the garden about 50 cm (20 in) apart, or directly into a suitable container (but remember that lovage grows about a metre tall). If you sow seeds in a seed box, plant them out when your seedlings are about 7.5 cm (3 in) high. Keep them watered well in dry weather – they don't like dry roots. The summer flowers produce oblong brownish seeds, which you can harvest for future planting just before they start to fall, by snipping off and drying the whole flower heads. Sift out any dried husks and stalks and store the seed in airtight containers.

DRYING

Lovage leaves are dried in the same way as parsley. Spread the leaves out on sheets of clean paper or on mesh in a shady, warm place where the air can circulate until they are dry – it should take a few days. When they are brittle, crumble them into airtight containers.

lovage, carrot and chicory salad

1 tablespoon finely chopped lovage leaves

1 large carrot, shredded into long curls using a potato peeler

1 firm unpeeled pear, shredded into thin strips using a potato peeler

12 chicory (or witloof) leaves, crisped in cold water and drained

3 tablespoons plain yoghurt

1 tablespoon mayonnaise

a squeeze of lemon juice

Toss the lovage, carrot and pear together and pile into the individual chicory leaves. Whisk the yoghurt, mayonnaise and lemon juice together and drizzle over the salad scoops.

Serves 4–6 as an accompaniment

marjoram

MARJORAM, SWEET MARJORAM *origanum majorana*

oregano

OREGANO *o. vulgare*

POT MARJORAM, GREEK OREGANO OR RIGANI *o. onites*

GOLDEN OREGANO *o. vulgare 'aureum'*

These two perennials are so closely related and their use in the kitchen is so similar that it is useful to discuss them together. In addition, while fresh marjoram and oregano are delicious with salads and mild flavoured foods, both have the best taste and greatest pungency when they are dried.

Like siblings, the differences between the two are subtle when they are young, and you can tell them apart more easily once they begin to mature. Sweet marjoram is a reasonably compact, shrubby perennial growing to about 45 cm (18 in) tall, with grey-green leaves that are small and soft. Its mildly savoury, almost grassy aroma is reminiscent of thyme.

Oregano is the assertive, older child; a bold, robust and densely spreading plant, thriving in most climates and growing to about 60 cm (24 in). It has rounder leaves that are covered by a down of fine hairs and a more piercing, almost peppery flavour. Both sweet marjoram and oregano have small, white flowers that form tight clusters at the tips of their stems – in Greece and Italy it is these very pungent dried flower tops that are mainly used in cooking.

You could safely add oregano to 90 per cent of Mediterranean recipes, as it relates perfectly to the food of that area. Therefore you'll find it in pasta and rice dishes, on pizza, in moussaka, avocado dip, tomato dishes, and with zucchini (courgettes), capsicums (bell peppers), and eggplant (aubergine). Greek oregano is usually sold in dried bunches packed in cellophane bags and is the most of pungent of all dried oregano, although the Australian-grown leaves have a similar intensity of flavour.

Oregano has even more potent qualities. It's a star on the antioxidant scene, ranking higher than even fruits and vegetables. The US Department of Agriculture says: 'oregano has 42 times more antioxidant activity than apples, 30 times more than potatoes, 12 times more than oranges, and 4 times more than blueberries. For example 1 tablespoon of fresh oregano contains the same antioxidant activity as one medium-sized apple.' So eat up!

Dried marjoram is a classic ingredient in herb mixes such as *bouquet garni* and *herbes de Provence*. Its subtle aroma makes it an ideal companion as it helps give body and depth but never dominates. Try it on its own with lightly cooked fish and vegetables, scrambled eggs, omelettes, savoury scones, dumplings and clear soups. The fresh leaves have some of oregano's pungency, and add an assertive quality to herb sandwiches and potato salad.

Fresh marjoram and oregano are readily available from fruit and vegetable retailers and in the fresh herb section of supermarkets. Sometimes they are prepacked in airtight containers and will keep well in these in the refrigerator for a week or more. If you buy loose bunches, put the stems in a glass of water to keep them fresh. Sprays of fresh marjoram or oregano can be wrapped in foil, sealed and kept in the freezer for some weeks. Or you can chop fresh leaves finely, mix them with a little water, and put them into ice-cube trays in the freezer.

GROWING

In your local garden nursery, you'll find variations of oregano and marjoram available as seeds and seedlings. Oregano is usually more piercing in scent, although sometimes it's hard to tell them apart – a puny oregano may resemble a healthy marjoram.

Oregano and marjoram will grow easily from cuttings. Take new shoots about 7.5 cm (3 in) long in late spring, when the young leaves have firmed enough not to wilt when placed in a pot of coarse river sand. Once they're well rooted, they can be planted out in pots, or put straight into the ground, leaving at least 30 cm (12 in) between them. It's also possible to grow them from seeds, although of course it's much slower. Sow the seeds in a seed box or pot in spring and plant them out into a sunny spot in the garden in well-drained soil when the seedlings are 7.5 cm (3 in) high.

Both marjoram and oregano should be harvested just before the plants are in full flower in the summer or early autumn. Both have a tendency to become woody as they get older, so to delay this as long as possible, it's a good idea to cut out the old wood at the end of winter before the new spring growth appears. You can be fairly ruthless with this and the plants will thank you with strong new growth. After about four years, the plants often become so woody that it is best to replace them.

DRYING

Cut the long stems, together with any flower heads, and hang them in bunches in a cool, airy place. The leaves tend to fall as they dry, so it is a good idea to enclose bunches in mosquito net, muslin, or a big paper bag with holes in it. When the leaves and flowers are crisp-dry, crumble them between your thumb and fingers to remove them from the stem. Store in airtight containers and they will keep their pungent flavour for months.

herbed roast potatoes

1 tablespoon virgin olive oil
2 large potatoes, peeled and cut into approximately
    2 cm (3/4 in) cubes
2 good sprigs fresh marjoram, about 25 leaves,
    finely chopped
1 clove garlic, finely chopped
 salt flakes, to taste

Preheat oven to 180ºC (350ºF). Spread the oil into a shallow ovenproof dish or baking tray. Using paper towel or a clean tea towel, remove excess moisture from the cubed potatoes. Spread them out in a single layer in the baking dish, sprinkle with the herbs and garlic, and bake in the hot oven for about 30 minutes. During that time, turn them once or twice so that all the edges are crisp and golden. Sprinkle with a good pinch of salt before serving.

Serves 2–3 as an accompaniment

lamb roast rub

The sumac tree produces crimson berries that are dried and pulverised to make a spicy powder. Its flavour complements tomatoes and avocado so well that we hardly ever eat them these days without sumac. In the Middle East it is widely used instead of vinegar or lemon juice as a souring agent sprinkled over kebabs just before cooking. And it is simply delicious combined with oregano on roasted meats.

1 tablespoon sweet paprika

1 teaspoon sumac

1 teaspoon dried oregano

¼ teaspoon ground black pepper

½ teaspoon salt

2 cloves garlic, peeled and crushed

Combine all the ingredients and rub well all over a leg or shoulder of lamb before roasting, for a full-bodied flavour and mouth-watering crust.

Makes enough for that lamb roast

MEXICAN OREGANO

At least two different kinds of plants are known as Mexican oregano – *Poliomentha longiflora* and *Lipia graveolens*. Neither is a true oregano. Mexican oregano is essential in *pozole*, a pork and hominy stew.

---

five-minute pizza

2 rounds pita bread

2 tablespoons tomato paste

1 teaspoon dried oregano

1 teaspoon dried marjoram

toppings to taste – try chopped cooked chicken, ham, capsicum (bell pepper), mushrooms, onions, peeled prawns or whatever you fancy

grated mozzarella cheese

Preheat the grill to a moderate temperature, about 180ºC (350ºF). Spread the pita breads with a generous layer of tomato paste and sprinkle over the dried herbs. Decorate the pizza base with whatever toppings you have on hand, and top with the grated cheese. Place the pizzas under the grill for 3–4 minutes, until the cheese is bubbling and browning in patches, by which time the pizza will be heated through. Serve immediately.

Makes 2

mint

SPEARMINT OR ENGLISH SPEARMINT *mentha spicata*

COMMON OR MOROCCAN SPEARMINT *m. spicata 'moroccan'*

APPLEMINT *m. rotundifolia*

Can anyone imagine a world without mint? A world with no mint sauce with the roast lamb, no fresh and minty-tasting toothpaste, no spearmint chewing gum, no after-dinner mints, and worst of all, no Minties for long car trips!

Mint crops up wherever there's an aroma issue – as breath fresheners, in toothpastes, chewing gums, mouthwashes, and even toilet cleaners. It's not a modern discovery, though – the Romans introduced the versatile mint family to Europe, where the leaves were initially used as an air freshener and insect repellent.

There are numerous varieties of mint, all with quite different flavours and scents even though they may look alike. One of the reasons for the diversity is that mints have a tendency to hybridise with each other, which is why the list of mint varieties continues to grow. Sometimes, as well as the flavour and aroma variations, there can be plain and variegated versions of the same thing.

Spearmint stands out from the crowd in the culinary department, followed closely by apple and ginger mints; their names describe the flavours and aromas.

Peppermint, which has a high menthol content and produces the true oil of peppermint, is mostly used medicinally and for herbal teas, but is not a regular in the kitchen due to a rather overpowering antiseptic character. It's useful for candy making, however.

Brush past eau de cologne mint in the garden and delight in the delicious fragrance that causes this decorative herb to find its way into potpourri. Its flowers are larger than most in the mint family and a deep shade of mauve, making them a pretty addition to mixed posies.

Pennyroyal with its creeping habit makes great ground cover in a shady part of the garden. While it's great as a flea-deterrent, it's definitely not for eating.

Vietnamese mint is not a mint at all, it's a *Polygonum* (see page 160).

It is spearmint, either fresh or dried, that gives flavour to mint sauce, as well as to mint jelly and mint julep. Chopped mint goes with hot, buttered peas the way tomato sauce goes with sausages, and gives a bright lift to new potatoes, and tomatoes too. A few fresh leaves on buttered bread with cream cheese make delicious sandwiches. Mint is a versatile herb, as much at home with ice-cream, sorbet and cheesecake as it is with roast or minced lamb and Middle Eastern salads.

Spearmint is an absolutely indispensable ingredient throughout the Middle East and Mediterranean, where it is used either fresh or dried. It gives its distinct aroma and taste to meat and vegetable dishes, to tabbouli, to yoghurt sauces, to soups and to salads. In Morocco, where mint is known as *naa naa*, spearmint is used to make mint tea, said to be the nation's most popular beverage. Mint is also used in tagines and kefta (ground meat grilled on skewers or made into a meatball stew). Dried or fresh leaves are used in the making of koftas and kebabs in India, as well as a cooling yoghurt raita.

Several types of mint are used in Thailand (where it is called *saranay*) and in Vietnam as a salad, a garnish and an ingredient of certain curry pastes.

Applemint, as the name suggests, has a strong scent of apples. You can mix the chopped leaves into fruit salads and fruit jellies, or include them in the batter for Asian-style deep-fried bananas.

Fresh spearmint is the one that's readily available from fruit and vegetable retailers and the fresh herb section of supermarkets. Opt for the smooth narrow-leaved English variety that has a better flavour for cooking if you have the choice. To keep it fresh, stand the bunch in a glass of water in the refrigerator. If you change the water every few days it will keep for a couple of weeks. You can freeze it using the ice-block method, and sprays of fresh mint may be wrapped in foil, sealed, and kept in the freezer for some weeks.

Spearmint butter can also be frozen and is delicious with lamb. Chop the fresh leaves, pound them into softened butter, allow to set in the refrigerator, then cut into squares and seal into small polythene bags or other suitable containers.

GROWING

English spearmint has elongated, smooth, bright green leaves, and the same pungent, warm flavour and aroma as its twin, common or garden or Moroccan spearmint, which has oval-shaped, crinkly, dark green leaves. Both are ideal for adding the finishing touch to the lamb roast. And both like a moist position in the garden or in a large tub under a dripping tap.

English spearmint is more difficult to grow than the crinkly-leafed variety. While the scent and flavour of English mint is clearer and stronger and its leaves have a finer texture, it is rather too susceptible to leaf-eating insects and thus something of a heartbreaker for the gardener.

Applemint grows approximately 30 cm (12 in) high, with oval, wrinkled, soft leaves and small white flowers that appear in autumn. Sometimes this variety is called pineapple mint.

This perennial herb has an overactive root system, and will completely take over your garden if you let it, so it is probably better off kept in control in a tub. Unlike many herbs, mint prefers a shady damp position. The shadier and damper the better it will thrive. If you want to plant it in the garden, put it into a 25 or 30 cm (10 or 12 in) plastic pot with the bottom cut out, and plant the entire pot. The pot will act as a barrier, preventing the runners spreading under the surface – at least, that's the theory – but sooner or later it will take over. Perhaps it's a good short-term method, if you're planning on selling your house within the next 12 months!

Propagate mint by root division, as even the smallest piece stuck in the ground will grow. Short stem cuttings taken after the new growth has hardened in late spring can be put straight into the ground, too, and roots will quickly form. It will grow from seed, but it's really never necessary to use this method.

Mint thrives in rich, moist soil, in semi-shade, but will also grow in poor, sandy soil if the ground is fertilised from time to time. Cut plants back to ground level in winter.

If your mint is attacked by rust, there's nothing for it but to dig out the plants, dispose of them and start afresh with new stock in a different part of the garden, or clean out the container and completely change the soil.

DRYING

Mint is easily dried. Cut the leafy stems just before they come into full flower and hang them in bunches in a dry, airy place. Make sure that when the crisp, dried leaves are stripped from their stalks they are kept in airtight containers, as this herb does not keep its full aroma and flavour if exposed to the air for long.

It's possible to dry mint in the microwave by placing the leaves in a single layer on a sheet of paper towel and 'cooking' on high for 20-second bursts, checking for crispness after each burst. As the leaves become dry to the touch, remove them, zapping only the remaining leaves until they too are dry. Stand a half a cup of water in your microwave with the leaves to prevent damaging the magnetron.

cool, refreshing minty drinks

Mint is a great flavour to add to summer coolers and frappés combining well with all sorts of fruits and vegetables including berries, melons, pineapple, apples and pears. To make a minty watermelon and blueberry cooler, blend about 400 g (14 oz) peeled and chopped seedless watermelon with 1/4 cup of blueberries, some ice-cubes and 2 or 3 mint leaves (more if you love the tang) until smooth. Serve with extra ice.

warm minted lamb and tomato salad

Inspired by Fiona Hammond's recipe for Lebanese Rolls with Minted Lamb and Tomato (*Good Food*, Text Publishing, 1998), this salad makes a refreshing light meal year round. The lamb fillets can be grilled or barbecued – we usually barbecue them. You can make it meatier or mintier, depending on the flavour you favour.

2 lamb fillets, each about 200 g (7 oz)
extra virgin olive oil
1 bunch fresh mint (the smooth narrow-leaved variety),
    leaves picked off the stems (use 2 if you really love
    that minty flavour)
1 punnet ripe baby tomatoes, halved
1 Lebanese cucumber, sliced
juice of 1 lemon
salt and ground black pepper to taste

To Serve
hummus
black olives
pita bread

Brush the lamb fillets with olive oil and cook them on the barbecue or under a preheated grill for about 3–4 minutes a side, or longer if you like your lamb well done. Remove from the heat, wrap each fillet separately in foil and set them aside to rest for 10–15 minutes. This is very important as it makes the fillets easier to slice thinly across the grain. After resting, slice each lamb fillet and place in a serving bowl with the torn mint leaves, tomato halves and cucumber slices. Toss the salad with a little lemon juice and salt and pepper to taste. Serve with hummus, black olives and pita bread.

mitsuba

cryptotaenia japonica

One of Japan's most widely used herbs, mitsuba, brings a tasty, aromatic flavour, not dissimilar to parsley, to clear soups, tempura, simmered dishes (*nabemono*) and steamed egg dishes such as the delicate custard known as *chawan mushi*. It is usually lightly blanched or added fresh at the last minute to retain its flavour.

The fresh leaves and blanched leaf stalks are also eaten in salads and sandwiches. Mitsuba is popular in Japan as a garnish: sometimes a few stems are tied into a knot close to the leaves, and the long ends trimmed off with a knife.

Traditionally it has always been grown as an early spring herb, but these days you can find it all year round in Japanese stores in the refrigerator section.

GROWING

Mitsuba has slim, sappy, dark green stems with three slightly serrated leaves on each. Its tiny star-shaped flowers quickly turn to seed. Related to the parsley family, it is also known as Japanese parsley, Japanese trefoil, trefoil and honewort.

Mitsuba is one of the few culinary herbs that thrives in both sunny and shady spots. In the right conditions, it grows to about 90 cm (36 in) in an upright, dense, spreading mound. For best results, plant seeds or seedlings in the spring in moist, rich soil in the garden. Keep watered and feed occasionally. For a continuous supply of fresh, young leaves, sow every six weeks thinning out seedlings to about 25 cm (10 in) apart.

Propagate by seed or root division.

mitsuba and tofu in clear soup

With thanks to food writer and chef, Hideo Dekura. Enjoy this very simple, very beautiful and very Japanese recipe. Serve with a deep bow.

4 squares of momen-dofu (hard tofu), each around
    3 x 3 cm (1½ x 1½ in)
8 mitsuba stems with leaves (use 4 leaves for
    making the stock)

Snapper Stock
300 g (10 oz) snapper bones or head
1 teaspoon sea salt
6 cups water
4 mitsuba leaves, torn in half
1 tablespoon Japanese soy sauce
1 tablespoon mirin
50 g (2 oz) fresh ginger, grated and squeezed to
    make ginger juice

To make clear snapper stock, sprinkle the snapper all over with salt and refrigerate for 20 minutes. Bring water to the boil in a large pan and add the fish and 4 of the mitsuba leaves, torn in half. Simmer gently for 30 minutes then strain through a fine sieve into another pot to make clear stock. Discard the bones.

Add soy sauce and mirin to the snapper stock and simmer for around 5 minutes. Remove from the heat and add the ginger juice.

Heat the tofu pieces gently in warm water. Place one in each serving bowl and pour over the clear soup. Garnish each bowl with the remaining mitsuba leaves.

Serves 4

mountain pepper

tasmannia lanceolata

Australia's unique contribution to the world of herbs and spices packs a pretty powerful punch. Mountain pepper is both a herb and a spice – that is, both the leaf and the berry are used. A native of the eastern seaboard rainforests of Tasmania, Victoria and parts of south-eastern New South Wales, you will find this bush growing at altitudes up to 1,200 metres (4,000 feet) – hence the name 'mountain' pepper. It is not to be confused with the big *Schinus* species of pepper tree often found shading a corner of the school-yard.

Mountain pepper has glossy, dark, leathery, elliptical leaves, which can vary in length depending on where they grow, and range from around 2 cm (3/4 in) in alpine areas up to 13 cm (5 in) down on the lowlands.

Fresh, dried or powdered, the leaves, berries and fresh flower buds all have a distinct woody fragrance and flavour, albeit at varying intensities.

If you're a lover of pepper, you could get very excited about this Australian version. But watch out, as the heat has a lingering quality – building on your palate for some minutes after you taste it. You might have a moment to regret your enthusiasm before the heat begins to recede!

The dried leaves have a soft woody fragrance along with a hint of pepper and dry, cinnamon-like notes. The flavour is similarly woody until its sharp pepper taste and lingering heat become apparent

The leaves can be dried and used in much the same way as bay leaves for a peppery flavour. You can buy powdered mountain pepperleaves from gourmet delicatessens and herb and spice specialists. A little goes a long way, so buy only small quantities. In addition, it's not a herb that retains its flavour well once ground, even under optimum storage conditions.

The ground leaves are ideal for infusing in olive oil for dipping crusty bread or for drizzling over soup or polenta. Extra virgin olive oil infused with mountain pepperberries and whisked with just a dash of balsamic vinegar makes an unforgettable dressing for salads.

And as for pepperberries, as Ian said in *Spice Notes*, 'only the brave, foolish, or taste-bud-deficient would entertain putting ground mountain pepperberries directly onto food; they are just so hot and numbing, that when not cooked, the flavour attributes cannot be fully appreciated'.

So take a tip from us and introduce these berries into slow-cooked casseroles and hearty stews, where the flavour can be best appreciated. They are excellent with game meats and, used very, very sparingly, in marinades for red and white meat. And how much should you add? Well, Ian's rule of thumb is to use about one-tenth the quantity you would use of conventional pepper.

You can occasionally buy frozen mountain pepperberries, but they are more readily available as a coarse-ground, oily looking black powder.

Dorrigo pepper (*Tasmannia insipida*) is related to mountain pepper. From the botanical name it's easy to deduce that the flavour is likely to be less aggressive – insipid, in fact – but possibly making this one a better starting point for the uninitiated.

GROWING

Mountain pepper is an attractive tree for a large garden, growing to about 4 or 5 metres (13–16 feet), albeit slowly. It likes a moist climate and well-drained fertile soil in a semi-shaded position with plenty of water. The new growth is a striking deep red and the tree bears creamy-yellow flowers in summer, which produce the black fruit or seed pods we know as mountain pepperberries.

This rather fascinating primitive flowering plant is a dioecious species. This means that it bears male and female flowers on separate plants and if you want to harvest pepperberries you will have to grow one of each.

DRYING

Pick a handful of leafy stems, making sure they have lost their newborn red glow, as the young leaves won't dry successfully. They can be dried in a hanging bunch, or the leaves can be snipped off and dried on a rack.

The berries also dry successfully on a rack, and of course, once they're dry, store them in airtight, clearly labelled containers.

mountain pepperleaf blends

Mountain pepperleaf blends well with other Australian herbs and spices to sprinkle over meats before roasting or barbecuing.

When making a herb blend, be adventurous, experiment and choose proportions of these ground herbs and spices to please your palate. Here are two of our favourites. Use the measures we suggest as a starting point for your own culinary adventures.

Kangaroo Fillet Blend
½ teaspoon ground mountain pepperleaf
1 tablespoon ground coriander seed
½ teaspoon roasted and ground wattleseed
½ teaspoon akudjura (ground bush tomato)
½ teaspoon salt

Lemon Pepper Blend
½ teaspoon ground mountain pepperleaf
½ teaspoon ground lemon myrtle leaf
1 teaspoon salt

mustard greens

BLACK MUSTARD *brassica nigra*

BROWN OR INDIAN MUSTARD *b. juncea*

WHITE OR YELLOW MUSTARD *b. alba*

Mustard has been around since Adam was a boy – or at least, since Alexander the Great was a boy. Back then, 'eat your greens' meant tucking into mustard leaves and if you were feeling poorly, your physician might very well prescribe a dose of mustard seeds. Moving forward a couple of millennia, they are still very much around.

Mustard seeds that are sprouted with cress in punnets for making mustard and cress sandwiches are the same ripened seeds that are collected for grinding to make the smooth or grainy mustards that add bite to beef. There are three types – black, brown and yellow (or white) – but the most popular for mustard greens and sprouts are the black and brown varieties.

Bright green mustard leaves have a pungent, peppery flavour and can be steamed, sautéed or simmered or added to salads where they make a sharp, tangy contrast to other salad greens.

Our ancestors may have been partial to the strong, biting flavour of the steamed leaves on their own, but for a piquant taste with wider appeal add a few leaves at the last minute when cooking spinach. You can also throw in a few leaves when you're making any kind of vegetable stock or soup. If you are growing your own mustard greens, simply pick the leaves as required.

To add a touch of colour to salads, opt for the variety known as 'Red Giant' with its reddish purple leaf that you can pick year round.

The Japanese mizuna (*B. juncea 'Japonica'*) has elegant, slender leaves, lazily serrated, with a sweet, fresh flavour – absolutely perfect for salads.

GROWING

Black mustard is a tall, upright annual growing to 2–3 metres (6½–10 feet) with branching stalks that bear smooth, bright green, pointed leaves with notched edges.

Brown mustard grows to about the same height, though its large oval leaves are not as pungent. They bear small yellow flowers, bunched tightly together, throughout summer, and it's from these that the seed-bearing pods evolve.

Yellow or white mustard seeds grow the same way, but the leaves are less inspiring for culinary use.

Mustard germinates quickly and has green shoots within a week of sowing. Sow seeds in the spring, 30 cm (12 in) apart in a sunny, open position. To grow enough to harvest your own seed crop, just scatter the seeds over your garden plot. You'll need to plant a few crops throughout the year if you want leaves to pick year round.

Mustard is often planted for its alkaline properties, which will counteract too much acid in the soil. The crop is also good for ground that has been damaged after too much mineral fertiliser, but continual planting depletes the soil. If you're addicted to those tasty leaves, move your crop around to rest the soil.

DRYING SEEDS

For harvesting the seeds, wait for the pods to swell, then pick them and allow them to dry out. Remove the seeds, and if necessary dry them further before storing in clean, dry, airtight, labelled containers.

SPROUTING

The important rule for sprouting is to not allow the seeds to dry out, while at the same time, not drowning them. You can grow mustard and cress on wet blotting paper, or in a glass jar with a piece of gauze, stocking or light fabric stretched across the opening and held in place by a strong rubber band. Run some water into the jar, swill around to wet the seeds, then drain it off, placing the jar on its side. Repeat this twice a day as the seeds sprout, and when the jar is full of delicious, succulent, living morsels, empty it out and start again.

summer salad greens with creamy mustard dressing

2 cups mixed salad greens, including oakleaf lettuce, sorrel, mizuna, young mustard greens, cress, rocket, salad burnet, chives, basil and chervil

$\frac{2}{3}$ cup plain yoghurt

1$\frac{1}{2}$ tablespoons white wine vinegar

2 teaspoons grainy French mustard

Rinse the salad greens and pat dry in a clean tea towel. Arrange on a platter, with the lettuce on the base and the smaller herbs on the top. Whisk the yoghurt, vinegar and mustard together, and drizzle over the salad just before serving.

Serves 2 as an accompaniment

myrtle

myrtus communis

This true myrtle is no relation to crepe myrtle or lemon myrtle. It is a dense, evergreen shrub whose small, glossy, oval leaves have a sweet, spicy orange fragrance. For centuries, shepherds in Mediterranean countries have made fires from myrtle wood to flavour roasted meats and game birds.

If you have myrtle growing in your garden, try placing a handful of fresh, young leaves under pork or lamb for the last 10 minutes of cooking time in the oven or on the barbecue. Or stuff a few fresh leaves inside roast pork while the meat rests before your carve it. Dried, the fragrant leaves and flowers are popular for making potpourri, sweet bags and herb pillows.

Top green salads or fruit salads with myrtle buds or the starry white flowers, or use them as a garnish for desserts, although you need to remove the bitter green part first. Season meats with ground dried berries for a delicate, peppery flavour.

GROWING

Myrtle is an erect, evergreen shrub usually growing to 3 metres (10 feet), but sometimes taller. It can be used for hedges or container plants, and because trimming keeps the plants compact, they can be clipped into formal ball or pyramid shapes, if you're so inclined. From late spring the shrubs are a swoon-inducing haze of fragrance: tiny five-petalled white flowers, almost hidden by prominent gold stamens, burst into flower from tightly folded white buds in a day. In late summer when the petals have dropped, the fruit begins to form, and gradually turns blue-black with a delicate whitish waxy bloom.

Myrtle thrives in a sheltered position in full sun or semi-shade with well-drained, medium-rich soil. Although it's hardy, it appreciates a dose of fertiliser occasionally, and a drink in dry weather.

To propagate, divide woody cuttings into 12–15 cm (5–6 in) pieces, trim off any side shoots, and press each piece into a deep pot of river sand, leaving one-third of the wood exposed at the top. Keep well watered. When the cuttings have made strong roots, they can be planted out. You can take tip cuttings, late in summer, in the same way as for hardwood propagation. If you want to start from scratch, sow seeds in the spring in prepared trays. When the seedlings are sturdy and have a good root system, plant them out in the garden as single specimens, group them together as a hedge, or plant them in tubs.

DRYING

Cut flowering stems in the morning and hang in bunches in a dry, shady place, or spread them out on a sheet of paper or on drying racks. When moisture-free, strip the flowers and leaves from their stalks and store in airtight, labelled containers.

Pick the berries when they appear and air-dry on a gauze rack or on sheets of paper in a warm, dark place. When completely dry, store in an airtight, labelled jar. Grind in a peppermill, or crush in a mortar and pestle just before using.

pandan leaf

pandanus amaryllifolius

Colour is one of the key attributes that the pandan brings to a dish, as well as its subtly sweet flavour. It always reminds us of our time living in Singapore, when we discovered that a bright grass-green pandan cake – a sponge topped with green, jelly-like icing – would be just the thing for our daughter Sophie's birthday cake.

The leaves used in cooking come from the fragrant screw pine tree, which is a palm-like evergreen. It looks like something you'd see in a B-grade sci-fi movie, with masses of stilt-like aerial roots supporting stiff branches. The leaves are spirally arranged, rather resembling the blades on palm fronds.

Tiny, fragrant, white flowers are followed by huge fruit heads up to 30 cm (12 in) in diameter that look rather like green pineapples and are in fact aggregations of berries.

The tough, fibrous leaves have been put to good use wherever the screw pine grows: they've been used for house thatching, woven into sails, and made into clothing, floor mats, and baskets. The grass skirts worn by Pacific Island women are often made from split, bleached pandan leaves. The fruit is edible but only after being cooked to neutralise the noxious qualities.

In cooking, the fresh whole pandan leaves are either crushed or boiled to extract the flavour and colour. Strips of fresh leaf flavour rice while it is cooking and are sometimes woven into baskets for serving glutinous rice or canapés – the ultimate dinner party tour de force. You can bruise a few fresh leaves, tie them in a knot, and add them to soups or curries during cooking, much as you can with lemongrass.

A rather eye-catching barbecue finger-food can be made by marinating bite-sized pieces of boneless chicken in some Asian spices then wrapping them in a piece of pandan leaf. Secure the parcel with a toothpick and barbecue – your guests can unwrap their own morsels, and they'll think you're wonderful.

The male flower cluster has a strong perfume that verges on the sickly-sweet. It is available as an essence or concentrate called Kewra essence – sometimes called the 'vanilla of the East' – that is added very sparingly to certain Indian sweets. On festive occasions, essences of rose and pandan deliciously flavour the spicy rice dish, biryani.

Store fresh pandan leaves (available from Asian grocery stores) whole in a plastic bag in the freezer. Carefully dried leaves (to retain the colour) are either chopped into pieces large enough to remove after cooking or powdered finely so that the texture is no longer fibrous. Sometimes you can buy the bright green spice powder from specialty shops. Dried pandan leaf is sometimes sold as *rampé* (Sri Lanka), or *daun pandan* (Malaysia and Indonesia). Store in a cool, dark place to retain colour and flavour.

GROWING

The screw pine grows to about 15 metres (50 feet) in tropical and sub-tropical climates in coastal and swampy areas from Madagascar, across South-East Asia, throughout the Pacific Islands and in tropical Australia. Because the trees tend to lean at an angle, they often look windswept and somewhat shorter than they really are.

Screw pines make a decorative (and practical) addition to a seaside garden. Plant them in warm, damp areas in full sun or part shade in moist, well-drained soil. When it's young, a pandan makes an attractive houseplant, all you have to do is give it plenty of water and remove any dead or damaged leaves. As a houseplant, you can help it to survive winter in less tropical areas. Propagate from seed soaked for 24 hours before planting or by detaching root suckers.

DRYING

Once you have your pandan tree growing, you can just pick the leaves as you require them. Drying them is tricky because you don't want to lose the colour and flavour. Use the usual drying method, spreading out on mesh or paper, but make sure the area is completely dark. The cavity of a roof is ideal, as is the cupboard that houses your hot water system. Once they are perfectly dry, store the leaf pieces in a dark, airtight container. To make use of the green colouring, put some dried leaves in the blender and process until you have a fine powder.

coconut rice cooked in pandan leaves (nasi lemak in pandan leaves)

This rice dish is a favourite of chef and food writer, Carol Selva Rajah, and is a lovely accompaniment to her Whiting Fillets Grilled in Turmeric Leaves (see page 159). The coconut rice will be aromatic and lightly flavoured with pandan. Carol recommends cooking it in the microwave.

2 cups long-grain jasmine rice
2 fresh green pandan leaves, washed
3 cups water
1 cup light coconut cream
salt to taste

Wash the rice in a basin of water, rubbing the grains lightly between the palms of your hands. It is important to rinse the rice in many changes of water to remove the starch then drain it thoroughly.

Holding the washed pandan leaves, in one hand, run a fork from top to bottom so that the leaves shred all the way down. Add the shredded pandan leaves to the rice – tied neatly into a knot if you like – where their juice and flavour will be released during cooking.

Combine the water and the coconut cream in a deep ceramic (microwave-safe) bowl, stirring well, then add the rice and pandan leaves and a little salt to taste if you wish. Microwave on high for about 35 minutes or until all the water is absorbed, then stir with a fork. Remove the pandan leaves before serving.

Alternatively, place the rice and other ingredients in a rice cooker and follow the cooking instructions.

Serves 6

pandan-flavoured coconut pancakes (kueh dadar)

Carol Selva Rajah tells us that traditionally these pancakes were served as long, cigar-shaped rolls tied with a pandan leaf bow and served warm with green tea or fresh lemon tea.

Filling

150 g (5 oz) grated palm sugar

pinch of salt

3/4 cup water

1 pandan leaf

1 cup desiccated coconut or fresh coconut

1 lime rind, cut into very fine julienne strips

Coconut Pancakes

3 pandan leaves shredded with a fork (see instructions in
   recipe opposite)

1 cup plain (all-purpose) flour, sieved

pinch of salt

 270 ml (9 1/2 fl oz) coconut milk

130 ml (4 1/2 fl oz) water

1 egg

butter or oil for frying

Garnish

coconut cream

To make the filling, place the sugar, salt, water and pandan leaf in a heavy saucepan and cook slowly, stirring constantly until the sugar dissolves. Add the coconut and stir over a low heat until the mixture is sticky. Remove the pandan leaf, then add the lime rind and set aside to cool while you make the pancakes.

To make the pancakes, pound the shredded pandan leaves with a tablespoon of water in a mortar and pestle, strain the green juice and set aside. Place the flour and salt in a large mixing bowl. Stir together the coconut milk and water then whisk it into the dry ingredients, together with the egg, to form a smooth, lump-free batter. Stir in the pandan juice, to colour the batter green.

Melt a knob of butter or oil in a hot frying pan. Add 2 tablespoons of batter and swirl around the pan to form a pancake. Flatten with a spatula and cook until the pancake firms and the edges start to brown. Flip the pancake over and cook the other side for around 30 seconds, or until golden brown. Transfer to a warm oven while you make the remaining pancakes.

When serving these pancakes as a dessert you have two options. Either you can fold the pancakes into quarters with a tablespoon of filling in the centre. Or, if you want to be traditional, make up long cigar-shaped portions of the filling to be inserted in the centre of each green pancake and rolled up tightly. Tie each pancake roll with a pandan leaf bow and serve with coconut cream.

Makes 8 pancakes

parsley

CURLED PARSLEY *petroselinum crispum*

ITALIAN OR CONTINENTAL PARSLEY *p. crispum neapolitanum*

If you are looking for a herb to grow under a dripping tap or in a damp corner of the garden then you can't go past parsley. The most common ones are the curled varieties that are perfect for garnishing and the flatter, darker Italian or continental parsley with its more concentrated flavour.

There are about 30 varieties of curled parsley, all with bright green, tightly curled leaves. Some, like the triple-curled and moss-curled varieties, are more crinkled and tightly curled than others. *P. crispum*, the one we are all most familiar with, is widely used for garnishing because of its decorative leaves. Italian parsley has deeply cut and serrated leaves like the tops of celery or lovage, is widely used in Middle Eastern and Mediterranean food, has a more concentrated flavour, and grows in large prolific clumps.

Parsley's taste could be described as fresh and crisp and perhaps a little earthy. It is also unassertive which makes it a perfect partner in mixtures with other herbs such as *fines herbes* (with chervil, chives and tarragon), or in a *bouquet garni* (with a bay leaf and a spray each of thyme and marjoram). Anyone who has grown parsley will know how prolific a healthy clump can be, so will understand why it's used by the cupful in some recipes ... it's because it's THERE!

Parsley leaves are at home with many savoury foods – in fact there is not one savoury dish that comes to mind that would be spoilt by the addition of parsley. Old-fashioned and very traditional, parsley jelly can be served with all white meats, particularly fish and chicken. Crisp-fried curly sprays of parsley are delicious with fish. Finely chopped Italian flat-leaf parsley stalks and leaves are the main ingredients in tabbouli, along with plenty of fresh mint. Italian parsley is indispensable in Middle Eastern cooking in tagines, combined at times with coriander and in chermoula – a marinade of herbs, oil, spices and lemon juice – served with meat or fish.

If you buy fresh parsley, look for bunches with firm stems and upright, springy leaves. Store in a glass of water covered loosely with plastic wrap. For freezing, chop fresh leaves finely, mix with a little water, and put them into ice-cube trays in the freezer. Sprays of fresh parsley may be wrapped in foil and frozen.

GROWING

When you're choosing a spot to plant parsley, remember it can thrive in areas that don't have the best drainage, and the moist soil will in fact delay the 'going to seed' cycle. Plant parsley in the garden in full sun or semi-shade, or in a pot on a sunny exterior windowsill or balcony. Just remember not to let the soil dry out. The main rule is to plant parsley in its permanent position, as its long taproot does not like to be disturbed.

Curled parsley can be tricky to grow from seed – there used to be a saying that parsley seeds go to the devil and back three times before they come up. They sometimes take two weeks to germinate, and during this time the bed *must never* be allowed to dry out, or the seeds will stop germinating altogether and you'll have to start all over again. Covering the seeds with up to 12 mm (½ in) of soil will help retain moisture in the ground for a longer period.

For Italian parsley, sow seed any time of year except mid-winter, directly into the garden where the plants are to grow, thinning out later to approximately 7.5 cm (3 in) between plants. Italian parsley is easy to grow. Three to four days after sowing, the seeds will usually germinate, provided that they are very lightly covered with soil to not more than 6 mm (¼ in) in depth, and kept moist.

Parsley plants will live for two years, especially if you cut the long flower stalks as they appear to keep them from going to seed during the first year. However, the second year's growth is never as good, and we prefer to sow seed each year to ensure strong and healthy plants.

DRYING

Parsley can be cut for drying at any time. It will keep its green colour and flavour if it's dried quickly in a warm oven preheated to 120°C (250°F). After turning the oven off, spread out the parsley heads, which have been snipped from the stalks, on a large tray or baking dish, and leave in the oven for 15 minutes, turning several times until crisp-dry. Store them in airtight containers away from the light.

penne with a sauce of parsley, prosciutto and pine nuts

Parsley is the perfect partner for pine nuts and prosciutto in this fresh-flavoured sauce to serve with penne or your favourite pasta shapes.

½ cup parsley leaves, loosely packed
juice of 1 lemon
2 tablespoons grated parmesan cheese
2 tablespoons roasted pine nuts
½ cup virgin olive oil
salt to taste
10–12 slices prosciutto
500 g (1 lb) penne pasta
100 g (3½ oz) bocconcini, cut into small cubes

Combine parsley, lemon juice, parmesan and pine nuts in a blender and process with the motor running. Gradually add the olive oil until a thick creamy pesto is formed. Add salt to taste.

Brush the prosciutto with a little extra oil and cook under a preheated grill until crisp. Set aside to cool, then break into pieces.

Cook the pasta in a large saucepan of boiling salted water until *al dente*, then drain through a colander and return to the pan. Stir in the parsley pesto and mix well. Toss over low heat until well combined. Spoon into warmed bowls and serve topped with the bocconcini and prosciutto pieces.

Serves 4

pennywort

centella cordifolia

INDIAN PENNYWORT *hydrocotyle asiatica*

Believe it or not, pennywort actually did exist before the current affairs television shows got hold of it in the late 1990s and dubbed it the 'arthritis herb'. It's a cheery little plant, easy to get along with and always happy, as long as you remember that its other name is swamp pennywort, for obvious reasons. Growing only 12–15 cm (4¾–6 in) high, it has leaves shaped like a rather rounded fan, or like a penny with a cut towards the centre. While thinking of pennies and cents, and the Latin name *Centella*, the leaves range from about the size of a two-cent coin to about the size of a penny.

Pennywort is not really what we could classify as a culinary herb. In Africa, the dried and powdered leaves are used as a kind of snuff. For many centuries, it has been used in India and Asia as a medicine for all sorts of things, which we won't delve into here. However, it's worth mentioning that there is anecdotal evidence that three leaves a day have been know to ease the pain of arthritis – but bear in mind that the scientific evidence to back it up is still lacking.

You can pick the leaves and eat them directly from the plant, or tuck them into a salad or herb sandwich. To disguise the flavour (not really necessary, but some people are fussy), sandwich the leaf between two small slices of cheese.

Drying is not recommended for pennywort.

GROWING

This herb has a delightful trailing habit that makes it a natural for a hanging pot. Leaf stems sprout at intervals from the thin, prostrate stems, and at each leaf point, roots will sprout if there is ground available for them. Therefore it will happily run all over your garden if you let it – which is a good reason to keep it in a pot.

Once you have obtained a root from a friend, a nursery or someone's garden, this little plant will be unstoppable. Just cover the root with moist potting mix, keep it watered, and it will grow. Frequent picking will keep the plant nicely dense – less frequent picking and inadequate water will lead to long, straggly strands.

A pot is recommended because of its spreading habit – we met a man who had filled an old cast-iron bathtub with soil and had a bath full of pennywort!

purslane

portulaca oleracea

Edible green purslane is a sappy, succulent herb from the *Portulaca* family. Gardeners like its red stems and stalks in herbaceous borders, especially when combined with the contrasting golden-leaved *P. sativa*. The latter is also edible, but is not as hardy as the green variety.

In the past, older shoots were cooked as a 'pot herb' (herbs used like vegetables for the flavour and nourishment in their leaves, roots and stems), and the pickled stems spiced up winter salads. But for many years, purslane seemed to fall out of favour, and lost its place in herb books. However, its culinary and nutritional benefits have recently been rediscovered – it is loaded with omega-3 fatty acids and is rich in antioxidants. The smooth, small, juicy leaves have a refreshing, zesty lemon tang and make a pleasant surprise to crunch on in a mixture of salad greens. With rich food, purslane's astringent properties help cleanse the palate.

Purslane is found on just about every continent. It's one of the world's most common useful wild plants (or weeds, depending on your point-of-view). Like okra, it contains mucilage, making it useful to thicken soups such as the French *potage bonne femme*. The green purslane most commonly used is thought to have come from the Middle East where you will find it in the salad *fatoush* and the cooling Armenian cucumber and yoghurt salad.

In Australia, early settlers tucked into cooked purslane as a substitute for spinach – hence the term 'poor man's spinach'. Try it with a little nutmeg grated on top. Sometimes thick stems of mature plants are sliced and pickled for the winter store cupboard. In Asia, the juicy stems and leaves with their ever-so-slight glutinous mouth-feel are dipped in fish sauce and eaten raw and added to stir-fries.

Purslane doesn't keep well, so it's best to buy and use it on the same day. Choose fresh-looking bunches, cut off the roots and stand the stems in a glass or stainless steel container. Avoid aluminium containers – the oxalic acid in purslane reacts with alloys in the same way that spinach does. Blanch for a few minutes in a stainless steel saucepan, rinse thoroughly and leave to cool to reduce the jelly-like texture before using.

HARVESTING

Purslane is eaten fresh and does not dry well. If you are growing it, gather 5–7.5 cm (2–3 in) leafy stems as you need them for making salads. When it's starting to look a bit hen-pecked, cut the plant low and after a short time it will produce a fresh crop of foliage. After repeating once more, the original plant will be depleted and the new crop of purslane, having been sown earlier, should be ready to pick.

GROWING

The juicy leaves are attached to short stems growing from a round, succulent, red stalk and the whole plant has a prostrate, sprawling habit. Tiny yellow flowers cluster on the branches in mid-summer, opening only at noon. Each bloom is followed by a seed case packed with thousands of tiny black seeds. Dig some compost or rich loam into light, well-drained soil and sow seeds from late spring to early autumn in a sunny position 15–20 cm (6–8 in) apart.

Keep the weeds away, water it well and the leafy stems will be ready to pick in four to six weeks. Gather purslane before it flowers, then after one or two pickings cut it back and it will shoot again. Successive seed sowing every two to three weeks is recommended so that new plants come on when the first ones have finished.

purslane with a neopolitan flavour

This makes a good brunch served on sourdough toast for those 'home alone' times.

1 bunch purslane (about 30 stalks)
1 tablespoon virgin olive oil
1 small onion, finely chopped
1 clove garlic, crushed or finely chopped
2 rashers bacon, rind and fat trimmed, finely chopped
2 tomatoes, peeled and chopped, seeds included
salt to taste
freshly ground black pepper to taste

Rinse the purslane and roughly chop into thirds; set aside. Heat the oil in a heavy-based pan and add the onion, garlic and bacon. Cook until the onion is transparent, then stir in the tomatoes. Cook a further 2–3 minutes, adding salt and pepper to taste. Add the purslane and stir through. Cover the pan and simmer for about 5 minutes, stirring occasionally.

Serves 1

rocket

eruca sativa

SALAD ROCKET *eruca sativa*

Salad rocket with its unique peppery flavour is *the* essential ingredient at any number of good sidewalk cafes. It's found layered with roasted vegetables in magnificent doorstep-sized sandwiches; lurking under stacks of char-grilled chicken and eggplant (aubergine); in, on and under hand-made pasta; and it constitutes the bulk of green mesclun salads in place of 'old-fashioned' lettuce.

Salad rocket (also known as arugula, ruchetta and roquette) is a branched plant with spear-shaped, torn-looking leaves with a mustardy, almost cress-like, tang. Culpeper called it 'rocket cress' or 'garden cress'. It is a great 'grow and pick' plant that you can harvest throughout the summery months, leaf by leaf.

It is sometimes confused with sweet rocket, *Hesperis matronali*, because they are part of the same big *Brassicaceae* family and both are referred to as rocket. Don't be misled by that adjective 'sweet', however, which refers to its fragrant single or double white, purple, or variegated flowers that perfume the air on warm evenings. The leaves of sweet rocket are too acrid for eating.

When you're buying salad rocket, look for firm, fresh, green leaves. If the leaves have a sickly, yellowish hue, you'd be better off going without. Store as you would lettuce, in a plastic bag in the crisper in the refrigerator. Rocket will only keep for a day or two, so it is best to buy it the day you want to use it. Rinse it well under running water, as the leaves tend to collect dirt as they grow. Drain well and gently pat dry with a clean tea towel.

GROWING

Salad rocket is often seen growing wild, but the cultivated herb has larger, milder tasting foliage and grows to around 90 cm (36 in). For crisp salad leaves, grow rocket fast. To do this, the plants will need a fair bit of 'tender loving care' to become established. The key ingredients for speed growing are rich soil that can absorb moisture, regular watering, a good liquid fertiliser and at least six hours of sun a day. A good way to check whether your rocket needs more water is to push your finger into the soil around the base of the plant; if it's not moist then water it.

Plant seedlings or sow seed in the spring directly into the garden. Seeds take about three to four days to germinate and the rocket should be ready for picking in about six to eight weeks. The very young leaves are a long oval shape, so be careful not to mistake them for weeds. The ragged serrations only develop as the plant matures.

Rocket flowers in mid- to late summer, and the small blooms are creamy yellow, or pale white with purple streaks. To collect the seeds for planting next season, allow them to ripen when the petals have fallen, then cut the stalks and place them, seed-heads first, into a paper bag so that the seeds will be collected as they fall.

When the leaves of the salad rocket are big enough, around 10 cm (4 in), begin to pick them from the outside of the plant. Young leaves are particularly tender. Gather leaves repeatedly until the plant begins to flower. Rocket is not a herb for drying and storing.

rocket pesto

1 bunch rocket

2 cloves garlic, chopped

½ cup raw macadamia nuts

¼ cup grated parmesan cheese

2 tablespoons extra virgin olive oil

a squeeze of lemon juice

salt and freshly ground black pepper to taste

Combine the rocket, garlic, macadamia nuts and grated parmesan in a blender and process. Add the olive oil a tablespoon at a time, blending well after each addition, and finish with a squeeze of lemon juice. Scoop the mixture into a bowl and stir until smooth, adding salt and pepper to taste.

Makes about 1 cup

snowpea, rocket, capsicum, avocado and basil salad

Select the smallest, sweetest snowpeas (mangetout) and fresh, young rocket leaves for this combination of flavour, colour and texture suggested by food writer, Lisa Lintner, who effortlessly transforms the simple into the sensational.

2 large red capsicum (sweet pepper)

300 g snowpeas (mangetout)

1 bunch rocket or 2 cups rocket leaves, washed

1 large ripe avocado

2–3 basil leaves

Dressing

2 tablespoons balsamic vinegar

4 tablespoons extra virgin olive oil

1 clove garlic, finely chopped

10 basil leaves, finely sliced

salt and freshly ground black pepper to taste

Halve the capsicum and remove all the seeds and the white ribs. Brush the halves with a little olive oil, place them on a foil-lined tray under a hot grill until the skins have blackened, then put the capsicums in a sturdy paper or plastic bag and set aside until they are cool enough to handle, 10–15 minutes. Remove the skins and slice the halves lengthwise into 1 cm (½ in) wide strips.

String and blanch the snowpeas in boiling water, then drain and refresh in ice water.

Cut the avocado lengthwise into half, then gently twist to separate. Remove the seed, peel off the skin and slice the flesh into thin wedges.

To make the dressing, combine all the ingredients in a lidded jar and shake well to combine. Taste for seasoning and adjust if necessary. Arrange all the ingredients attractively on a large platter, sprinkle over the dressing, top with 2–3 extra whole basil leaves and serve.

Serves 6–8 as an accompaniment

rosemary

UPRIGHT *rosemarinus officinalis*

PROSTRATE *r. prostratus*

A sprig of rosemary will enhance just about anything – even memory, if the saying 'rosemary for remembrance' is to be believed. Every year as Anzac Day approaches, rosemary bushes around Australia and New Zealand are trimmed to provide sprigs for adorning lapels on this special day of remembrance.

A lamb roast simply isn't complete without sprigs of rosemary and slivers of garlic stuffed into slits on the outside and, if you really want to go to town, liberally dusted with sumac and sweet paprika before roasting.

Hardy, sun-loving, perennial rosemary is one of the most pungent herbs of all. There are two main varieties, both with delicate blue flowers and long, narrow leaves that are dark green on top and silver-striped underneath. Upright rosemary's leaves grow to over 2.5 cm (1 in) long, and have the better flavour. The leaves of low-growing or prostrate rosemary are smaller and narrower. But no matter which variety you opt for, the warmly vital, freshly resinous taste and aroma adds a delicious, savoury tang to all types of meats and most vegetables.

Although it is famously paired with lamb, rosemary can be used in pâtés, sauces for pasta, with eggplant (aubergine), zucchini (courgettes), lima beans ... basically, the rule is: 'Think Mediterranean, think rosemary!'

Years ago at Somerset Cottage we made rosemary scones for visitors (you simply stir a tablespoon of finely chopped leaves into a plain scone mixture before adding the liquid). The flavour was subtle and piquant, and when served hot from the oven and freshly buttered, they disappeared like – well – like hot scones!

If you pick more rosemary than you need, or have leftover stems from a bought bunch, fear not, it keeps well for a week or so in a jug of (regularly changed) water. The ice-cube trick works well too, or sprays of fresh rosemary may be wrapped in foil and frozen for some weeks – but if you have a growing rosemary plant, why bother freezing it?

There's a real technique to stripping fresh rosemary leaves from the stem. Always hold the stem by the bottom in one hand and with the thumb and forefinger of the other pluck off each leaf in an upward motion. That impulsive downward action will tear off some of the coarse outer stem bark, which doesn't add anything to a dish.

GROWING

Rosemary thrives in a Mediterranean-style climate, which means dry conditions, hot dry summers, a small amount of rain and in a spot that is sheltered from wind. Plant in a sunny, well-drained spot in sandy or alkaline soil and hold back on the watering. It loves tubs.

Upright rosemary with its stiff, bushy habit grows to about 1.5 metres (5 feet) and is ideal for hedges. Trim frequently to encourage growth and prune after flowering. Prostrate rosemary is rather more ornamental than culinary, making a thick, matted ground cover, or hanging fetchingly over the edge of retaining walls. It is excellent in rockeries and also in tubs, where it will spill toward the ground in a most attractive way. We have seen prostrate rosemary planted on a sloping bank sweeping down to a swimming pool, where the blue of the flowers and the blue water seemed to reflect one another. Both varieties start blooming in the autumn and continue on through the winter until spring.

Rosemary is fairly easy to grow from 15 cm (6 in) tip cuttings. For best results, take cuttings late in winter and plant them in a pot of clean river sand or potting mixture. A dip in rooting powder is helpful, too. Once

Top to bottom:
Rocket Pesto (recipe page 134);
Apple, Mint and Horseradish Cream
(recipe page 78);
Aioli with Lemon Myrtle (recipe page 75)

Risotto with Garlic and Fennel (recipe page 67)

the roots have formed, you can transplant it to the garden or a larger pot. You can also grow upright rosemary from seed (in the spring is best) in a prepared seed box, planting out when the seedlings are about 7.5 cm (3 in) high, and leaving about 60 cm (24 in) between plants.

The prostrate variety can only be propagated by cuttings or by layering, which is an easy process described in the 'Down to Earth' section. If you're a more haphazard gardener, the same result can be achieved by putting half a brick or a rock onto the stem to keep it pressed against the garden soil. When the layered branch has developed a good root system, just cut it away from the parent bush and plant out in a sunny position.

DRYING

Cut the branches before the plant begins flowering (when the flavour is at its best), shaping the bush at the same time. Then hang in bunches in a shady, airy place, with cloth or newspaper underneath to catch the falling leaves. Strip the dry leaves from the stalks, crumbling them into small pieces. Stored in airtight containers, the flavour will remain strong over a long period. Dried rosemary can also be added to potpourri for scenting clothes and deterring moths.

rosemary scones

I have made so many thousands of scones over the years, that I usually make them by 'feel' rather than by following a recipe. Just for the record, here's my recipe for rosemary scones measured out. However, 'feel' is very important when making scones and you may need a little more flour or a little less milk to achieve the correct 'firm but moist' consistency.

1 cup self-raising flour
70 g (3 oz) butter
pinch of salt
2 teaspoons chopped fresh rosemary (about 2 sprigs)
1/3 cup whole milk

Preheat the oven to 200ºC (400ºF). Process the flour, butter and salt in a food processor, or rub with your fingertips until you achieve the consistency of breadcrumbs. Stir in the chopped rosemary, and gradually add the milk, to achieve a firm but moist consistency. (You may not need the entire 1/3 cup, or you may need a little more – it depends on the flour.)

Sprinkle a little extra flour onto the workbench, turn the scone mixture out, and lightly pat out to a thickness of about 2 cm (3/4 in). Cut into squares or circles about 3 or 4 cm (1 1/2 or 1 3/4 in) in diameter, and place on a flour-dusted oven tray. Bake for about 10 minutes, until the scones have risen and the tops are lightly browned. They should separate easily into top and bottom halves with gentle finger pressure; you should never cut scones. Serve them warm with a small dab of butter melting into each half.

Makes about 10 scones

sage

salvia officinalis

FRUIT SALAD SAGE *s. dorisiana*

PINEAPPLE SAGE *s. elegans*

Sage is a pungent herb with an aroma that's fresh, head-clearing and balsamic. It's one of those 'a little goes a long way' herbs with a flavour that rarely diminishes over long cooking times.

The silvery grey of the leaves and the bluish-mauve flowers, make common sage (*S. officinalis*) a welcome variation amongst the greens of most other herbs in the garden. When the leaves are young, they are soft, downy and pale green, but like Dickens' Miss Haversham; as they mature the colour fades, and the original softness becomes a rough-textured leaf surface, rather like a cat's tongue. Sage flowers are like miniature snap dragons, and you'll probably see bees paying great attention to these sweet morsels. In this hardy perennial's native home, Dalmatia, the honey from sage flowers is renowned.

As poor Jemima Puddleduck found to her peril, sage and onions makes the ideal stuffing for roast duck, as well as for other rich, fatty foods such as pork, chicken and oily fish. And as a bonus, its 'grease-cutting' qualities will aid digestion, or so they say.

Think of sage when you think 'big' flavours like full-bodied pea, bean and vegetable soups; hearty winter stews; dumplings; meat loaf and roast meats. Like most herbs, you can also add a judicious amount of chopped sage to vegetable and egg dishes. It is a traditional ingredient in mixed herbs, along with thyme and marjoram, and is currently fashionable deep-fried and served as a garnish.

We always include a small amount of sage when we make herb sandwiches, making sure the sage is about 10 per cent of the quantity of milder herbs like parsley, chives and chervil.

Fresh sage is readily available from fruit and vegetable retailers. Avoid bunches that look wilted unless you're really desperate. Stand the stems in a glass of water, changing the water every second day, and enjoy fresh sage for a week or so. You can also buy dried sage leaves crushed or powdered. The crushed leaves are the most flavoursome.

The *Salvia* family to which sage belongs includes some 900 species of annuals, perennials and soft-wooded shrubs, but the herb sage, *S. officinalis*, is the one with the real culinary qualities. Fruit salad sage has edible pink flowers that make a delicious addition to cordial, salads and fruit salads. Pineapple sage has edible red flowers that bloom prolifically from early summer through autumn; pick them off the stem and suck the delicious nectar straight from the flower.

GROWING

This hardy, erect perennial grows to about 90 cm (36 in) with a base that becomes rather woody after a couple of years. As a rule of thumb, plants with woody stems and slightly greyish coloured leaves, such as sage, thyme, rosemary and oregano, like reasonably dry conditions, and they don't like to have wet feet. So pick a very sunny, slightly elevated (if possible) spot for your sage in sandy, well-drained soil. Sow the seed in spring (in mild climates you can sow in autumn as well) directly into the garden or in a prepared seed box if you prefer. Plant your seedlings out when they are about 10 cm (4 in) tall, leaving 60 cm (24 in) between each.

Although the seedlings need care and water, let the mature plants enjoy dry spells as nature intended. Sage will also grow from cuttings or layering – have a look at Ian's section on growing for more details (see 'Down to Earth' page 162).

As your plant ages, prune out the dead twigs so that it doesn't get too woody, too soon. Pruning every week in the summer may be a good idea, but ultimately it depends on how vigorously the plant is growing.

Because sage is a perennial, it is always available for picking. Like other herbs, the ice-cube method works if you want to do it.

DRYING

Harvest sage for drying just before the plant flowers. Either tie loosely bundled long sprays together and hang them in a cool, dark, airy place, or lay the branches out on racks to dry in a warm position, but never in direct sunlight. Once dried, pull off all the leaves and store them in airtight containers immediately.

It is unwise to leave the bundles, attractive though they are, to gather dust. Rubbed sage leaves will never feel as crisp as many other dried herbs due to their high oil content and the downy structure of the leaf. Dried sage makes one of the tastier herbal teas.

french-style stuffed pumpkin

½ cup fresh white breadcrumbs

1 whole pumpkin, about 20–25 cm (8–10 in) in diameter

1 tablespoon butter

1 large onion, very finely chopped

pinch of salt

pinch of pepper

pinch of nutmeg

1½ teaspoons fresh sage, chopped

½ cup gruyère cheese, grated

2 cups pouring cream

Preheat oven to 120ºC (250ºF). Spread the breadcrumbs out on an oven tray and place in the oven for about 15 minutes to dry out. Meanwhile, cut the top off the pumpkin, and scoop out all the seeds and fibrous strands. Place the cleaned pumpkin in an oiled baking dish and set aside. Increase oven heat to 200ºC (400ºF).

Melt the butter in a pan and sauté the onion over medium heat until transparent. Add the dried breadcrumbs and seasonings, including the sage. Cook for another minute or so, then remove from the heat. Stir in the cheese, then spoon the mixture into the pumpkin cavity. Pour in enough cream to come to within a centimetre of the top. Fit the lid back on to the pumpkin.

Bake for about 1½ hours until the outside of the pumpkin is beginning to soften. Reduce heat to about 160ºC (325ºF), and continue baking for another 30 minutes until the flesh is tender. If the pumpkin looks as though the outside is burning, wrap it lightly in foil. Present the whole pumpkin at the table, then remove the lid and spoon out the filling.

Serves 4–6

salad burnet

sanguisorba minor

Salad burnet is a fresh-is-best herb, just as its name implies, and by rights it should be as popular as other salad herbs such as rocket and chicory. Add whole sprays of this cool, light, refreshing, soft herb to a tossed green salad, or float individual leaves in fruit punches and drinks. Chop the small, serrated, cucumber-flavoured leaves into cream cheese to make a dip; or use the whole leaves in sandwiches with cottage or ricotta cheese, or as a garnish for any dish that needs a touch of green. It is a tasty topping for scrambled eggs, particularly when mixed with a few sprigs of chervil, if you have some on hand.

Sometimes you can buy bunches of salad burnet from fruit and vegetable retailers. When available, buy the day you plan to use it, as it is rather prone to wilting. Wash salad burnet and store it in the crisper drawer of your refrigerator, as you would lettuce.

If you are growing your own, pick leaves just before you need them. To freeze for drinks, pull small leaves from the stalks and put them whole into ice-cube trays. Top up with water and freeze. Salad burnet doesn't dry well, and loses its appeal when dried.

GROWING

This delicate perennial grows to about 30 cm (12 in). It has a weeping, fern-like appearance and was often used as a border plant in traditional knot gardens. Its leaves are small, round, serrated and spaced about 2.5 cm (1 in) apart in pairs of 10 or 12 on each side of a slender stem. As the stems become long and heavy, they fall outward from the centre, so the more you pick it from the outside edge, the better. In summer, reddish pink, berry-like flowers appear on long stalks that shoot up from the centre.

Sow seeds (or plant seedlings) in the spring in their permanent position as salad burnet does not like being moved. Keep the ground moist while the seeds are germinating, then, when the seedlings are about 7.5 cm (3 in) high, thin them out to 30 cm (12 in) apart. As salad burnet is a soft salad herb and wilts quickly in hot, dry weather, keep it well watered at this time. It has no particular soil requirements, is very hardy, and will grow strongly all through most winters.

Salad burnet scatters many seeds that germinate easily, so it is advisable to cut the flower heads off as the stalks begin to lengthen, or it will take over the garden.

pear salad with salad burnet and borage flowers

This recipe is perfect for single servings or arranged on a platter where people can help themselves.

2 ripe, firm pears (Packham or beurre bosc)
10 sprigs salad burnet
12 fresh borage flowers
a good quality vinaigrette, for dressing

Peel and core the pears and slice them lengthwise into long, slender wedges. Pick the leaves from 2 of the sprigs of salad burnet. Arrange the remaining salad burnet sprigs on a serving platter and place the pear slices on top. Sprinkle over the borage flowers and the picked salad burnet leaves, sprinkle with dressing and serve.

Serves 4

savory

WINTER SAVORY *satureja montana*

SUMMER SAVORY *s. hortensis*

Fresh or dried, summer and winter savory both add an appetising, peppery bite that doesn't overpower. It's good to have both types growing: summer for its fragrant, piquant, distinctive taste; winter for its compact, hardy nature and glossy green leaves.

Opt for savory whenever a peppery piquancy is called for. Beans, peas and lentils, however you prepare them, benefit from the savory touch and in fact its popular German name, 'Bohnen-kraut', means 'bean herb'. Savory is delicate enough to complement egg dishes and robust enough to hold up in slow-cooked casseroles, stews and hotpots. Mix fresh or dried savory with breadcrumbs to coat fish, pork, and veal fillets; add it to meat loaf and meat balls; or sprinkle over poultry or pork before roasting. A classic *fines herbes* blend will often include savory.

Fresh summer savory is available in season from specialty produce suppliers and keeps well provided you stand it in a glass of water in the refrigerator. If you change the water every day or so, it should last for a week or more. Its soft foliage may be frozen in ice blocks at any time or wrapped in foil and frozen. Winter savory freezes well, too. Wrap sprays of soft new growth in foil and freeze. It will keep well for several weeks this way.

Dried summer savory, which includes the flower tops, can be bought year round and needs to be kept in a cool, dark place.

GROWING

Summer savory is a small, slender, herbaceous plant with hairy branching stems that tend to snap easily. Often it will have a rather top-heavy, sprawling growing habit, as the soft stems struggle to carry the prolific burden of soft, greeny-bronze leaves. These small, oval leaves have a stronger flavour than winter savory.

Winter savory has tiny, lipped white flowers and a rather stiff appearance that makes it ideal for borders of low hedging.

There is also a decorative, prostrate variety of winter savory, *S. repandens*, which spreads in dense, cushiony mounds, and is useful for filling pockets in paved paths and patios. It's a great choice for hanging baskets, as the tiny branches will tumble enticingly over the rim.

Annual summer savory grows to about 45 cm (18 in) high and likes a sunny, well-drained spot. Plant seedlings in the spring or sow seeds by scattering them over finely dug soil in the garden where the plants are to remain. You can plant summer savory in containers if you prefer. Successive sowings may be started in spring and carried on into mid-summer, each crop being harvested just as the flowers begin to appear. When about 5 cm (2 in) high, thin out the seedlings leaving approximately 15 cm (6 in) between plants. Summer savory bears small pink, white or lavender flowers in late summer, which are often harvested with the leaves.

Honeybees swarm around savory when it is in bloom and it was traditionally grown near beehives. An old-time cure for a bee sting was to remove the sting and rub the spot with fresh savory leaves.

Winter savory can also be grown from seed in the same way. Alternatively, take small tip cuttings of new growth in late spring when the leaves have hardened, then put them in a pot of wet river sand until roots have formed. When you transfer them to the garden, allow 30 cm (12 in) between plants. Winter savory makes a good low hedge, but you'll need to group the plants closer together, about 20 cm (8 in) apart, to achieve this.

DRYING

Both summer and winter savory can be dried with good results by hanging them in bunches in an airy place just before flowering. When the leaves are crisp-dry, they are easily separated from the stalks by running the thumb and forefinger up and down the stems. Stored in airtight containers, the flavour will remain strong for a long time.

Summer savory's stronger flavour makes it more satisfactory for drying and most commercial growers prefer it for this reason.

broad beans with summer savory

Savory brings a distinctive peppery piquancy to this dish without overpowering the broad beans.

2 cups shelled fresh broad beans
4 sprigs summer savory
1 tablespoon butter

Place the beans and half the savory in a saucepan of salted, boiling water, and cook until just tender. Drain, discarding the savory. Return the drained beans to the pan with the butter and the remaining savory, stripped from the stems. Shake the pan over heat while the butter melts, toss well and serve immediately.

Serves 4 as an accompaniment

sorrel

FRENCH SORREL *rumex scutatus*

French sorrel is a leafy perennial that grows in thick clumps like spinach. Its broad, mostly smooth, oval leaves are approximately 15 cm (6 in) long and 7.5 cm (3 in) wide, and are joined to reddish stems, rather resembling thin rhubarb. It has a lively, tangy flavour that really brightens up a green salad and the leaves are the perfect shape for laying lengthwise in a baguette with tuna and salad.

In times past, sorrel was prepared and eaten just like spinach, often with the addition of well-beaten eggs and butter, or cream and a little flour, to bind it and mellow the sharp flavour. As sorrel has a different consistency from spinach, it softens and melts faster; you can simply blanch it or cook it very quickly in butter without any water at all and then chop or sieve it to make a purée.

There are several varieties of sorrel, mostly rather sour and acidic. The milder French sorrel with its refreshing, lemony sharpness is the one cultivated for culinary use. However, it contains oxalic acid and should be eaten in moderation as a side act rather than centre stage. Always use stainless steel utensils when cutting and cooking sorrel as iron or aluminium will react and cause unpleasant flavours.

The tang of torn, fresh sorrel leaves can almost make a salad dressing superfluous. They give a pleasant appetising bite to scrambled eggs, and add flavour to lentil, bean or country-style soups. But sorrel is probably best known today when made into a sauce and served as a heavenly accompaniment for fish, veal, lamb, pork or poultry, drizzled over hot boiled potatoes, or used as a filling for omelettes. You can even top a supermarket-bought quiche with home-made sorrel sauce to turn it into something really special.

You can buy sorrel in bunches from specialty fruit and vegetable markets and store it in the vegetable crisper of the refrigerator for up to a week. If you are growing sorrel in the garden, a few plants will provide tangy leaves for salads all year round. It is rarely processed and doesn't keep its flavour well when dried.

The fresh leaves are available throughout the year in moderate climates. Whole, washed young sorrel leaves may be carefully wrapped in foil, sealed down with the fingers at the edges, and frozen for some weeks.

Sorrel, long a valued pot herb, would have been gathered wherever it was found growing wild, to be taken home and put into bubbling stews, or mixed with other green leaves, for salads. It has a reputation for sharpening the appetite and English diarist, John Evelyn (1620–1706), commented on its addition to salads, saying that it 'imparts a grateful quickness to the rest as supplying the want of oranges and lemons'.

GROWING

Sorrel is an easy, undemanding plant to grow, and it saddens me that whenever we stocked it in our herb nursery, we eventually had to plant it out into our own garden because no one wanted it. It grows prolifically in temperate areas in full sun or part shade in moderately fertile, well-drained soil with occasional applications of manure and a drink in dry weather. The small, greenish flowers appear in summer, near the top, and on either side, of long, rhubarb-like stalks. And never forget that snails and caterpillars are the worst enemies of succulent-leafed sorrel and are completely undeterred by the oxalic acid content. In fact they seem to thrive on it!

Propagation is by seed or by root division of the clumps in the autumn; but broken pieces of taproot will also shoot, which is worth remembering if you are tossing old plants onto the compost. Plant seedlings or sow seed in a prepared box in the spring. When seedlings are big enough to handle, plant them out, leaving 15 cm (6 in) between each one. Alternatively, sow seed directly into the ground where the plants are to grow, thinning out to 15 cm (6 in) apart when they are about 5 cm (2 in) high. In summer, as soon as the flower stalks begin to rise, they should be cut off at the base to prevent the plant from going to seed. If this is done, sorrel will continue to flourish for many years.

sorrel sauce

Serve this lemony sauce with pan-fried ocean trout fillets, or allow it to cool and serve it as a dressing with salads and cold meats. Add an egg yolk along with the cream to make a richer sauce.

1 tablespoon butter
50–60 g (2–2½ oz) young sorrel leaves, washed and
    chopped (about 50 leaves)
1 tablespoon flour
1 cup chicken stock
1–2 tablespoons cream

Melt the butter in a saucepan and gently cook the sorrel until soft. Blend in the flour and gradually add the chicken stock, stirring well until smooth; the sauce should have the consistency of thickened cream. Remove the pan from the heat and immediately beat in the cream. Don't blend the finished sauce to a smooth purée as the finely chopped sorrel gives the sauce a more interesting texture. This sauce can be frozen for up to 4 weeks.

Makes about 2 cups

tarragon

FRENCH TARRAGON *artemisia dracunculus*

Beware inferior imitators! French tarragon, with its unique, tart flavour and spicy anise aroma, is one of the most sought after culinary herbs. The leaves are long and narrow and grow on either side of thin, wiry stalks that, together with the main stems, twist and fall in a tangled way. The mature plant is quite thick and bushy, about 90 cm (36 in) high and wide.

A member of the *Artemisia* family, French tarragon is the only one that has culinary uses. Other *Artemesias* such as wormwood and southernwood, while still recognised as herbs, are much too bitter to eat, while Russian tarragon (*A. dracunculoides*), is flavourless and an unworthy substitute.

French tarragon is one of the four essential ingredients in the *fines herbes* mixture (the others being chives, chervil and parsley in equal quantities). The warming, aromatic fragrance of tarragon complements fish and shellfish, and it is an excellent herb to use with chicken, turkey, game, veal, kidneys, egg dishes, and in chicken or fish soup – French-style, of course!

Tarragon gives an air of elegance to all sorts of dressings and sauces, and to a green salad. Eggs Benedict just wouldn't be the same without it. Tarragon steeped in white vinegar could almost be rated 'the original and best' of all herb vinegars, and it is a useful ingredient for making your own mustard.

Fresh French tarragon stems will last for a few days in water, provided that it is changed every day. Be cautious buying it fresh – if there's no distinct anise aroma or tangy taste it's probably Russian or Mexican. Bright, hardy-looking yellow flowers are a dead giveaway of the Mexican variety, so leave well alone if you see them. If you want to freeze tarragon for future use, strip the fresh leaves from their stalks, chop them finely, mix with a little water, and put them into ice-cube trays in the freezer. Sprays of tarragon may be wrapped in foil and frozen for some weeks.

Alternatively, for making sauces, or using instead of sauces, finely chopped fresh tarragon can be mixed with softened butter. Once the butter has chilled, it can be cut into pieces to be wrapped separately in plastic wrap.

Mexican tarragon (*Tagetes lucida*) isn't an *Artemisia* at all. It is a cousin of those most familiar of summer annuals, the marigold, and is an altogether sturdier looking plant than true tarragon. Its firm, dark green leaves have a spicy anise aroma and flavour similar to French tarragon, which makes it a kind of a substitute. The Aztecs used it to flavour *choclatl*, their cocoa-based drink. Sadly, many fruit and vegetable retailers sell bunches of this plant under the guise of tarragon, and some inexperienced cooks are unaware that it is not the true French variety.

GROWING

With typically Gallic temperament, French tarragon can choose to disappear for no good reason, as many disappointed gardeners will attest. Perennial French tarragon likes well-drained soil and a sunny position. Although it doesn't mind slightly dry conditions, you will need to water it during a long dry spell. In late summer it produces small, tight, yellowish buds, but as they rarely open into full bloom, they do not set seed. If you're lucky enough to have it survive in your garden, it needs to be replanted every third year as the fragrance and flavour deteriorate over time. Propagating by cuttings is probably the best way to obtain new plants.

The true French tarragon is notoriously difficult to find in nurseries, so if you have one, your friends and acquaintances will be delighted if you share yours with them. Take 15 cm (6 in) tip cuttings in late spring when the new, soft leaves have become fairly firm. Insert the cuttings, which have had the lower leaves carefully removed, in a pot of coarse river sand, leaving approximately 5 cm (2 in) of cuttings above the sand. By mid-summer the roots should have become established enough for planting out in the garden – about 30 cm (12 in) apart. It also grows well in a pot in a sunny spot.

You can propagate by root division although this will not yield as many plants. Tarragon dies away to ground level in winter (except in very warm climates). The new shoots that appear early in the spring form a creeping root system and this is the time to strike. Sever 5 cm (2 in) long pieces of the main root, together with a new shoot, and plant 30 cm (12 in) apart. Within about two months these root cuttings will be roughly 45 cm (18 in) high. In very cold climates, it is a good idea to keep the roots covered in winter with grass clippings or straw.

DRYING

As tarragon withers away in winter, it is important to preserve the leaves when they are in abundance. Harvest as the flower buds appear until late autumn, just before the leaves begin to turn yellow. Hang the leafy stalks in bunches, or spread them out on wire racks for quicker drying, in a warm, dry, airy place. When dry, strip the leaves by running your thumb and forefinger down the stem and store them in airtight, labelled containers away from the light.

eggs benedict

Not traditional eggs Benedict, in that it uses a béarnaise sauce instead of the traditional hollandaise. Purists may wish to omit the tarragon from the recipe for béarnaise.

4 bacon rashers, rinds removed
4 eggs
2 English muffins, split into halves
Béarnaise Sauce (see recipe page 152)
French tarragon leaves for garnish

Grill or panfry the bacon until crisp, then set aside in a warm place. Poach the 4 eggs, and toast the muffin halves lightly.

To serve, place one muffin half on each plate, top with bacon and an egg, and pour the sauce over. Garnish with fresh tarragon and serve immediately.

Serves 4

béarnaise sauce

2 eggs, separated
90 g (3 oz) butter
1 tablespoon lemon juice
1 tablespoon fresh French tarragon

Separate the eggs and put the yolks in a blender. Whisk the egg whites to soft peaks. Melt the butter and lemon juice until just boiling. Switch on the blender and slowly pour the hot butter mixture onto the yolks; the mixture will thicken as the hot liquid cooks the yolks. Remove from the blender and stir in the chopped tarragon and whisked egg whites. This can be done slightly in advance and kept warm in a thermos.

Makes ½ cup

tarragon salsa

1 slice day-old bread, crusts removed
1 tablespoon tarragon vinegar
¼ cup tarragon leaves
¼ cup Italian parsley leaves
¼ cup virgin olive oil
1 clove garlic, crushed
salt and pepper
chilli powder (optional)

Place all the ingredients except salt, pepper and chilli in a food processor and process until finely chopped and blended. If necessary, add a little water to make the salsa a moister consistency. Add seasoning to taste and a pinch of chilli powder if desired. Store any unused salsa in a sealed container in the fridge for up to two weeks.

Makes about 1 cup

chicken breast fillet with tarragon salsa

2 tomatoes, peeled and seeded
1 large zucchini (courgette)
4 medium-sized mushrooms, wiped
3 tablespoons virgin olive oil
1 onion, finely chopped
1 teaspoon sweet smoked paprika
salt and pepper
4 chicken breast fillets, tenderloin removed
Tarragon Salsa (see recipe)

Chop the tomatoes, zucchini, and mushrooms into small dice and set aside. Heat a little of the olive oil in a frying-pan, add the onion and sauté until just tender. Add the diced vegetables to the pan with the paprika and continue to cook until the zucchini has just become translucent but is still holding its shape. Add salt and pepper to taste. Meanwhile, brush the chicken lightly with oil and cook on a hot barbecue or grill.

Serve the chicken on a bed of the tomato mixture, topped with tarragon salsa.

Serves 4

Rosemary's Glazed Pears (recipe page 8)

Chamomile Cooler (recipe page 38)

thyme

GARDEN THYME *thymus vulgaris*

LEMON THYME *t. citriodorus*

Got plenty of thyme on your hands? Tired old puns aside, there are countless varieties of thyme, most of them more decorative than culinary. Ornamental varieties such as Westmoreland, golden, variegated lemon, and pretty, grey 'silver posy' thymes may be used in emergencies, but their flavour is not as pungent, nor as true. There are also a number of creeping, mat-like varieties, but they have such interwoven, tiny branches that the tedious job of trying to disentangle a sufficient quantity for cooking is simply not worthwhile.

Good old garden thyme and lemon thyme have the most value in the kitchen. With very small greyish-green leaves on wispy thin stems, garden thyme has a big, generous flavour that enhances many dishes and is an essential ingredient in many herb blends, such as mixed herbs (with sage and marjoram) and *bouquet garni* (with parsley, marjoram and a bay leaf).

Its savoury, pungent flavour is indispensable in almost any savoury food. You name it; you can put thyme with it. A short list of special marriages partners thyme with minced beef in all its forms, with Mediterranean-style vegetables, roast potatoes, and marinated olives.

In the Middle East the word *za'atar* refers to thyme, and is also the name of a mixed herb blend consisting of dried thyme, sesame seeds, sumac (or sumach) and salt. We saw a scrubby little hardy plant growing on a harshly bare hillside in Turkey, which was identified as *za'atar*. It did look a little like our domesticated thyme and definitely had a thyme-like flavour.

Lemon thyme has slightly larger, softer and greener leaves, and an unmistakable lemony fragrance overlaying the typical thyme scent is released when they are crushed. The mild flavour is particularly in demand with fish and chicken, omelettes, asparagus and all kinds of food where a hint of lemon is appropriate. It is sometimes used as an extra ingredient in a *fines herbes* blend, with chervil, chives, parsley and tarragon.

Fresh thyme can generally be bought in small bunches from produce markets or fruit and vegetable retailers, and the bunch will keep for over a week in the refrigerator. If thyme is kept too moist it will blacken and lose its flavour.

As thyme's foliage is so tiny, we think it an unnecessarily laborious job to strip the stalks for freezing a few leaves in ice-cube trays, particularly when this herb dries so well. You can freeze whole sprays of thyme if you really want to.

Dried thyme leaves should be grey-green and free from any bits of stem as these don't soften in cooking.

GROWING

Garden thyme is a tough little survivor – those grey-green leaves tell you that, as do the hard, woody stems at the base of this bushy 30 cm (12 in) high plant. Like a small, noisy dog in next-door's yard, thyme delivers lots of punch for its size, and it's not to be ignored. The flowers are pinkish white and appear in spring in whorls at the tips of the branches. Lemon thyme has slightly larger and greener leaves and the spring-blooming flowers are deep pink. It has a spreading type of habit and only grows to about 5 cm (2 in) high.

Garden thyme has extremely small seeds. Sow them in spring into a prepared seed box, or scatter straight into finely dug soil, keep moist, and thin out later to about 15 cm (6 in) between plants. Propagating by root division is easy and can be done in spring. Alternatively, take tip cuttings approximately 10 cm (4 in) long in late spring, inserting them into a pot of river sand, and keeping them watered. This method ensures good root systems very quickly. Once it's established, garden thyme will grow better and have more flavour in dry conditions than if you pamper and fertilise it. Cut the bushes back hard at the end of flowering and renew them every two years or so.

Propagating lemon thyme from seed is not recommended, as the seedlings may not be as fragrant as the parent plant. For this reason, the seed is not readily available, and propagation is either by tip cuttings or root division. For healthy plants, cut them back after flowering has finished and start again with fresh plants every two or three years.

DRYING

The taste and aroma of garden and lemon thymes are much more penetrating when they're dried. Harvest the leafy branches just before they start to flower for fullest flavour, and gather them on a dry day before midday. Hang little bunches in a shady, airy place, and when crisp-dry, strip off the leaves and seal in airtight containers.

CHOOSING THE RIGHT THYME...

Thyme is another of those herbs like basil where, thanks to its popularity, nurserymen have had a field day. There are over 100 varieties (and many cultivars); new ones seem to be 'discovered' every year. Many are decorative, aromatic plants that are ideal for rockeries or ground covers with their tiny, entangled, dense foliage. Others are mainly a source for essential oil.

As common names seem to vary from place to place – and garden shop to garden shop – make sure you know the botanical name too. Other culinary thymes you may find in your local garden shop include:

CARAWAY THYME *T. herba-barona* – a tough, frost-hardy ground cover that combines well with meaty dishes

LARGER WILD THYME OR
BROAD-LEAVED THYME – *T. pulegoides* – can be used instead of common thyme in cooking

PIZZA THYME – *T. nummularius* – a dense ground cover combining oregano and thyme flavours that's popular with pasta and tomato dishes

WILD (OR CREEPING) THYME – *T. serpyllum* – another thyme that can be used instead of T. vulgaris

goat's cheese soufflés

We have Anneka Manning to thank very much for these sensational soufflés with good old garden thyme, from her book, *More Good Food* (Text Publishing, 2000). You can prepare the soufflés in advance and keep them in the refrigerator for up to 2 hours before baking. However, they will need about 5 minutes more in the oven if you make them this way.

a little melted butter

½ cup polenta (cornmeal) for coating

80 g (3 oz) butter

75 g (2¾ oz) plain (all-purpose) flour

2 cups milk

150 g (5 oz) soft goat's cheese, crumbled

1 teaspoon finely chopped fresh thyme leaves

4 egg yolks

salt and ground black pepper

6 egg whites at room temperature

Preheat the oven to 180°C (350°F). Brush the inside of 8 x 150 ml (5 fl oz) soufflé dishes with melted butter then coat with polenta, shaking out any excess. Place the dishes in a large ovenproof dish or roasting pan.

Melt the butter in a medium saucepan over medium heat. Add the flour and use a wooden spoon to stir until the mixture is smooth and beginning to bubble. Cook for 1 minute, stirring often. Remove from the heat and gradually add the milk, stirring until smooth and combined. Return to the heat and boil for 2 minutes, stirring constantly.

Remove from heat and stir in the goat's cheese and thyme. Spoon the mixture into a large bowl and set aside for 10 minutes to cool.

Add the egg yolks to the goat's cheese mixture and stir well to combine. Season to taste with salt and freshly ground black pepper.

Put the egg whites in a large bowl and whisk with an electric beater or balloon whisk until peaks form. Fold a large spoonful of egg whites into the goat's cheese mixture and stir until well combined. Gently fold in the remaining egg whites until just combined.

Divide the mixture between the prepared soufflé dishes. Add enough boiling water to the ovenproof dish or roasting pan to reach halfway up the sides of the soufflé dishes. Bake in a preheated oven for 25 minutes or until puffed up and golden.

Serves 8

turmeric

curcuma longa

Turmeric is familiar to most of us as the brilliant yellow spice with a pungent aroma that stains irrevocably when we spill curry down the front of our favourite shirt. If you find yourself in the Spice Bazaar in Istanbul, you'll discover that they tend to call turmeric Indian Saffron because of its ability to colour as dramatically as saffron – but at a fraction of the price.

Closely related to ginger and galangal, turmeric has bright green, lance-like leaves (similar to canna leaves) and forms clumps up to about 1 metre (just over 3 feet) high from its lumpy, orange-fleshed rhizome. Why is the harvested part a rhizome and not a root? Well, it's a bit of a fine line, but basically rhizomes are the finger-like parts that grow off the main tuber.

The large leaves can be shredded finely and added to curries and other dishes or used as a garnish, and are an important ingredient in Nonya and Indonesian cooking, especially in the spicy rendang meat dishes. In Thailand, the young tender shoots are gathered during the rainy season, and boiled as a vegetable served with *nam prik*.

Asian specialty stores tend to stock fresh turmeric leaves and the rhizomes, which can be added to Asian and Indian dishes for colour and flavour.

Store rhizomes as you would onions or garlic, in an open container in a cool dark cupboard. When peeling and chopping fresh turmeric, make sure you use gloves, and even then some of the oily circumin content will transfer to your skin and give you nicotine-y fingers for a couple of days.

GROWING

Turmeric is grown throughout tropical Asia but, like ginger, can successfully be grown in temperate area gardens in a warm, sunny position in well-drained soil. Coming from the tropics, turmeric likes to be watered and fertilised regularly.

Propagate by rhizome division in spring. To divide a rhizome, just break a finger with one or two buds (the daughter rhizome) from the main tuber, or you can re-use your original tuber (the mother rhizome) and even cut it in half lengthwise to make two plants. Plant them in sandy potting mix in a pot or tray until they have sprouted leaves and are large enough to transplant.

Turmeric can be grown in a pot, but remember the size and weight of the adult plant, and make sure your pot is at least 50 cm (20 in) deep so that there is enough weight in the pot to counter-balance the turmeric. After about eight months, when the lower leaves turn yellow, your crop will be ready for lifting. In the commercial world, the crop is dried and pulverised to produce the powdery spice we all know so well.

whiting fillets grilled in turmeric leaves

This delicious recipe is one of Carol Selva Rajah's specialities. A delicate fish like whiting works best with this subtle spice mix. It should be cooked slowly at first to allow the spices and the turmeric leaf to impart their flavour. In Malaysia, whiting is a delicacy and the fish would be cooked whole. Carol tells us that the fish would be eaten using fingers, so the bones can easily be removed and the flesh picked out and eaten with rice and sambals.

6 turmeric leaves, the length of each whiting fillet

1 tablespoon vegetable oil

1 teaspoon turmeric powder

6 whiting fillets

8 shallots or 1 red Spanish onion, roughly chopped

3 stalks lemongrass (about 8 cm/3 in of the thick, juicy end, roughly chopped

3 cm (1½ in) piece of fresh ginger, peeled

1 teaspoon chilli powder, or to taste

1 teaspoon cumin powder

2 tablespoons lime juice, to taste

salt and pepper

2 kaffir lime leaves, centre stem removed and thinly sliced

1 beaten egg

2 tablespoons coconut cream

Wash the turmeric leaves, then dry them well, rub with a little oil and wrap them in foil until ready to use. Sprinkle turmeric powder over the whiting fillets and set aside until ready to cook.

Put the shallots, lemongrass and ginger in an electric blender, or use a mortar and pestle to pound them to a paste. Add the spices and the lime juice and season with salt and pepper to taste. Stir in the kaffir lime leaves and beaten egg until well combined.

Soften the turmeric leaves by plunging them briefly in hot water, then lay them out on a clean work surface. Place 1 whiting fillet and 1 tablespoon of the herb and spice mixture on the centre of each leaf and top with a little coconut cream. Overlap each edge, and fix in place with a bamboo skewer. If the turmeric leaves do not hold fast you may have to wrap the made up parcels in a piece of kitchen foil before placing them under the griller to cook.

Preheat the grill to a medium temperature. Cook the whiting fillets for 6–8 minutes, turning over as each leaf turns brown. After about 5 minutes, or when the fish smells aromatic, turn up the heat to finish cooking for a further minute or so.

Serve with rice and a sambal made from coconut cream and thinly sliced kaffir lime leaves.

Serves 6

vietnamese mint

polygonum sp

Vietnamese mint is a bit of a phoney – it really isn't a mint at all, in spite of its peppery mint flavour. It's actually a *Polygonum*, which literally translates to 'many knees'. If you look at the purplish stems this makes sense, as there are little knee-like joints all along them, and roots can form at any of these spots.

The smooth leaves have an elegant spearmint shape, tapering to a long point, and on the dark green background there is a smaller darker shadow, as though someone has retraced the shape with a soft crayon. In open, sunny positions, this herbaceous perennial grows to 80 cm (32 in) high, and is topped with dense clusters of tiny white or pink blossoms.

Vietnamese mint's common name of 'knotweed' is an apt description of its swollen, jointed stems. There are over 200 species of *Polygonum*, most of them purely decorative.

Vietnamese mint, also sometimes called Asian mint or even Vietnamese coriander, is absolutely vital in the Malaysian/Singaporean laksa, and is an intrinsic part of most South-East Asian cuisine. In Thailand the shoots and leaves are eaten raw with *nam prik* or added to curries, while in Vietnamese cooking, they're used in salads or served with spring rolls. Finely shredded, the leaves make an excellent garnish.

You can buy Vietnamese mint in bunches from Asian specialty stores and some fruit and vegetable retailers. It will keep well for a couple of days in a glass of water in the refrigerator.

Pick and use fresh leaves as required. Vietnamese mint doesn't dry well, shrivelling down to nothing and losing its characteristic flavour.

GROWING

Vietnamese mint can be grown easily (almost too easily) in the garden or in a pot on the windowsill. Growing your own is a surefire way of ensuring consistent supply for most of the year, as it tends to be both prolific and rampant in the right conditions. In fact, if you place a few stems in a glass of water they will sprout roots within a few days. Plant the sprouted stems in a pot and let them establish until roots show from the drainage holes of the pot, then plant them out into the garden or a larger pot.

vietnamese mint and prawn salad

½ bunch Vietnamese mint, leaves picked

½ bunch coriander, leaves picked

1 punnet cherry tomatoes, halved

2 shallots, peeled and finely sliced

1 Lebanese cucumber, halved, seeds scooped out and sliced

2 teaspoons fish sauce

2 teaspoons sesame oil

juice of 1 lime

1 long red chilli, finely chopped, seeds removed

2 teaspoons palm sugar

20 medium king prawns, cooked and peeled

Place the Vietnamese mint and coriander leaves in a large mixing bowl with the tomatoes, shallots and cucumber.

To make the dressing, combine the fish sauce, sesame oil, lime juice, chilli and sugar in a mortar and pestle and mix well.

Spoon half the dressing onto the salad ingredients, and toss very gently. Divide the salad between four plates, top each serving with a few prawns and sprinkle over the remaining dressing.

Serves 4 as an entrée

down to earth

GROWING HERBS AT HOME

Tremendous satisfaction can be achieved by growing your own herbs and the wonderful thing about them is that they can occupy as much or as little space as you like.

Most herbs will grow as well in tubs and pots as they do in the garden, and a basic understanding of their requirements is all you need to grow them successfully.

Because the main objective when growing herbs is to have them on hand for everyday use in the kitchen, it is advisable to grow them in a spot that is close by. The ultimate 'kitchen garden', be it in the yard near the back door, in pots on a balcony or even in a window box in an apartment, is one that is accessible and enjoyed.

Herbs are pretty robust and have simple needs. After all, they have been around for millennia and have the ability to survive and prosper without our intervention. There are a few basic rules you need to follow to keep your herbs happy. Firstly herbs, like us, need sunshine and fresh air. We have rarely seen herbs grow well indoors so put them in a suitable position outside.

ANNUALS AND PERENNIALS

Many people have told us over the years that they have a completely 'brown thumb' and lament with comments such as 'I always kill my herbs, I don't know why I bother!'

What a lot of people are not aware of is the fact that a number of the herbs will only live for one season, and then die as part of their natural life cycle. These herbs are called *annuals* and a few which prosper for two years are called *biennials*. Herbs that do not die off after a season are called perennials, and the majority of *perennials* are reasonably robust looking shrubs.

Some annuals, such as coriander and basil, can't wait to grow up and bolt out in front of their peers to blossom early, flower prolifically, go to seed and then die. This seemingly inevitable fate can be arrested, although not indefinitely postponed. We suggest nipping these hormone-charged adolescents in the bud. Pick off the flower buds as soon as they appear. This will prevent them from flowering, then going to seed and finishing their life cycle.

Perennials are much easier to manage; however, they also need some care. Herbs such as thyme, sage, oregano and rosemary may become straggly and woody if they are not regularly harvested or pruned. At the end of summer, up to half of the foliage can be pruned from a perennial herb. This is the time to shape the plant, and rather than throwing the prunings away, dry the leaves to keep you going through winter when new growth will be slower to emerge.

SOIL AND GROWING CONDITIONS

Herbs are relatively undemanding, which is an endearing quality when one considers how much they give back to us in flavour, aroma and efficacy. Nearly all herbs like friable, well-drained soil that has been conditioned with good compost.

Don't bombard herbs with fertilisers and expensive nutrients; they won't appreciate them. It is fascinating to observe how many herbs, when grown in relatively poor soil on rocky Turkish hillsides, will have a stronger flavour than their lush, pampered city-living counterparts. It is a bit like those home-grown tomatoes that never look as good as the ones bought in the supermarket. But in reality, the flavour of these seemingly meagre offerings is far superior to the highly fertilised, over-watered and mass-produced product.

To grow herbs in pots, tubs and hanging baskets there are just a few practical pointers for success.

- Make sure the container is big enough for the root system of the herb you are planting. As a basic rule of thumb, for shrubs, the depth of the pot should equal the height of the plant. So if you are planting common garden thyme that will grow to about 20 cm (8 in) high, make sure the receptacle is at least 20 cm (8 in) deep. For shrubs such as bay trees, the depth of the pot can be approximately one-third of the height the tree will grow to.

- Always use a good quality potting mix, as proper potting mixes have been blended to have the optimum balance between water retention and good drainage.

- Put some pieces of broken pot or flat rocks in the bottom of the pot so it drains effectively and the soil is not washed out through the holes in the base.

- Place the pot in conditions that resemble the recommendations for the particular herb. Although most herbs need to be grown outdoors, their preferences range from semi-shade and well-sheltered to full sun and exposed to the elements.

- Most importantly, don't forget to water your pots. A herb in the garden will send its roots looking for moisture if you neglect it, and may just survive. A herb in a pot however is entirely dependent upon you to keep it watered. If the pot dries out completely, the roots have nowhere to go to look for moisture and the plant will die.

INSECTS

Many common insects have inordinately good taste and will love your herbs as much as you do. The trouble is they may get to them first – even at 'snail's' pace.

Using insecticides is not a good idea for culinary herbs because residues may be left which could be harmful to your health. Vigilance and the use of natural insect repellents can be just as effective and is safe. One of our family favourites is a garlic spray that Mum used to make and the recipe for it is very easy.

garlic spray

3 large garlic heads, unpeeled
6 tablespoons medicinal paraffin oil
1 tablespoon oil-based soap, grated
2 cups hot water

To make the garlic solution, roughly chop the garlic and put it in a blender with the paraffin oil. Blend together then scrape the resulting pulp into a bowl, cover and leave for 48 hours. Stir grated soap into hot water and stir until melted. Mix the soap and water into the garlic mixture. When cool, strain the solution into screw-top jars and store in the refrigerator.

To spray the herbs, add 2 tablespoons of garlic solution to 2 litres (4 pints) of water.

Remember to repeat spraying after rain, as the previous dose will be washed off.

PROPAGATING HERBS

You can buy herb plants from a variety of retailers. Nurseries and garden centres tend to stock the most complete ranges of herbs, while supermarkets and greengrocers will often sell them as well. Ask the assistant if the herbs have been 'outside hardened' as it is common for some mass producers to put plants on sale that have come straight to the megastore from an igloo (a kind of hothouse shaped like, well, an igloo) or glasshouse. These protected hothouse specimens can suffer from shock when exposed to the real world and once again you will erroneously blame your 'brown thumb'.

Once you have some herbs growing, a lot of satisfaction can be gained by propagating your own.

There are four main types of propagation: root division, taking cuttings, layering and sowing seeds.

ROOT DIVISION

Herbs like mint and pennyroyal will spread and grow into sizeable clumps, so one way to keep them healthy and to propagate more plants is to divide them up. This is easily achieved by digging up the clump, carefully separating say a 20 cm (8 in) root system into 5 smaller clumps of 4–5 cm (1½–2 in) and simply replanting.

CUTTINGS

Growing plants from cuttings is an ancient form of propagation, which involves taking a piece of plant material and growing roots on it. Cuttings are most appropriate for firm-stemmed herbs like rosemary and the process is quite straightforward.

When taking cuttings (striking) from a parent plant, always keep them in water or wrapped in a damp cloth until ready to put into sand. Be sure they do not wilt. Use coarse river sand firmly packed into a pot for striking cuttings, never use beach sand as it is too fine and more than likely has residues of salt in it.

Take tip cuttings of reasonably firm growth about 10 cm (4 in) long, cutting the stem just below a leaf node with a sharp knife or secateurs. Remove the leaves from the lower 4 cm (1½ in) that will be put into the sand and leave at least a third of the foliage on the top. When preparing cuttings, always pull off leaves with an upward pull, or use secateurs, to avoid tearing the bark on the cutting.

Never push cuttings into the sand, as this will damage the end and hinder the chances of making a successful strike. Always make a hole first using a skewer or pencil that is slightly thicker than the cutting. Moisten the ends of the cuttings and dip the bottom 1 cm (1/2 in) into a suitable cutting powder (available from nurseries). Shake off excess powder and insert the lower third of the cutting into the hole in the sand. Try to cover at least two leaf nodes (the part where you carefully pulled the leaf off) and press the sand firmly around the cutting. Flood with water and be sure to keep cuttings moist *at all times*.

Place the pot (which may have many cuttings in it as long as they are about 2 cm (¾ in) apart) in a semi-shady spot, so the sun's rays do not dry out the sand too quickly or burn the cuttings.

After several weeks, depending upon the weather, the cuttings will have formed roots and can be separated and placed into separate pots to become established before re-planting into larger pots or out in the garden.

LAYERING

Propagation by layering works on the same principle as taking cuttings, however you don't cut the stem off the host plant until it has formed roots.

Layering works best for plants that send out horizontal stems, or ones that can be easily bent down to ground level.

Select a length of stem and bend it down towards the ground. Trim off the leaves 5 cm (2 in) on each side of the part that is touching the ground in exactly the same way as you would for a cutting.

Moisten a couple of leaf nodes, dust them with cutting powder and then bury them up to 2 cm (¾ in) below the surface. It is a good idea to push a little hoop of wire over the stem and into the ground to stop the stem from springing back out of the ground when you turn your back.

Keep the area well watered and again, in several weeks you can pull up the layered stem, cut it off the plant and it can be grown from its own, newly developed root system.

SEEDS

When sowing seeds always keep the seedbed moist at all times, as drying out, even for a short period, may cause germination to cease. A pot about 20 cm (8 in) in diameter or a shallow trough filled with a 50/50 mix of river sand and soil is ideal.

Put the container on a level surface, as accidental over-watering or heavy rain can wash all the seeds to one end.

Tamp the sand-and-soil mix down flat with a small piece of wood and make furrows in the surface about 4 mm (¼ in) deep.

Sprinkle the seeds into the furrow; ideally there should be a few millimetres space between each seed.

Cover the seeds, making sure there are no lumps in the covering sand-and-soil mix.

Tamp the surface down again and give the whole surface a good soaking watering, but do it gently so the seeds are not disturbed or washed away.

When the seedlings are about 5 cm (2 in) high, carefully remove them from the seedbed and re-pot into individual pots before replanting in larger pots or in the garden when appropriate.

index